W9-ADF-797

Molly Fowler
The Dining Diva

Presents

Menus for Entertaining

Food Photographs by Mike Bowlin

Molly Fowler, The Dining Diva, Presents Menus for Entertaining

Copyright © 2007 Molly C. Fowler

All rights reserved. No part of this book may be reproduced in any form or by any electronic or mechanical means including information storage and retrieval systems without permission in writing from the publisher, except by a reviewer, who may quote brief passages in a review. This book contains recipes collected over many years from family and friends and adapted during years of catering.
Permission requests should be directed to:
Molly C. Fowler
P.O. Box 40446
Houston, Texas 77240-0446
www.thediningdiva.com

Disclaimer
The recipes in this book have been carefully tested by our kitchens and our tasters. To the best of our knowledge, they are safe and nutritious for ordinary use and users. For persons with food or other allergies or those who have special food requirements or health issues, please carefully read the suggested contents of each recipe carefully and determine whether they might create a problem for you. All recipes are used at the risk of the consumer.
We will not be responsible for any hazards, loss, or damage that may occur as a result of any recipe use.
For those with special needs, allergies, requirements, or health problems, please consult your medical advisor before using any recipe.

IMPORTANT: Pesons who may be at risk from the effects of Salmonella poisoning (pregnant women, the elderly, young children, and those with impaired immune systems) should consult their doctor with any concerns regarding the consumption of raw eggs.

Library of Congress Number: 2007934012
ISBN: 978-0-9798597-0-0
First Printing 2008

Food Photographer: Mike Bowlin
of Mike Bowlin Photography
5773 Woodway, #405
Houston, TX 77057
mbfoodphotos@gmail.com

Cover Design by Ira Van Scoyoc

Layout, Design and Digital Editing by Ira Van Scoyoc
By Grace Enterprises

Project Manager: P. Van Scoyoc
By Grace Enterprises
P.O. Box 1456
Manvel, Texas 77578
www.ByGraceEnterprises.com

Copy Editing by Shirin Wright and J. K. Fowler

Printed in China

Menus for Entertaining

To Jennifer —
Bon appetit!
Molly Fowler

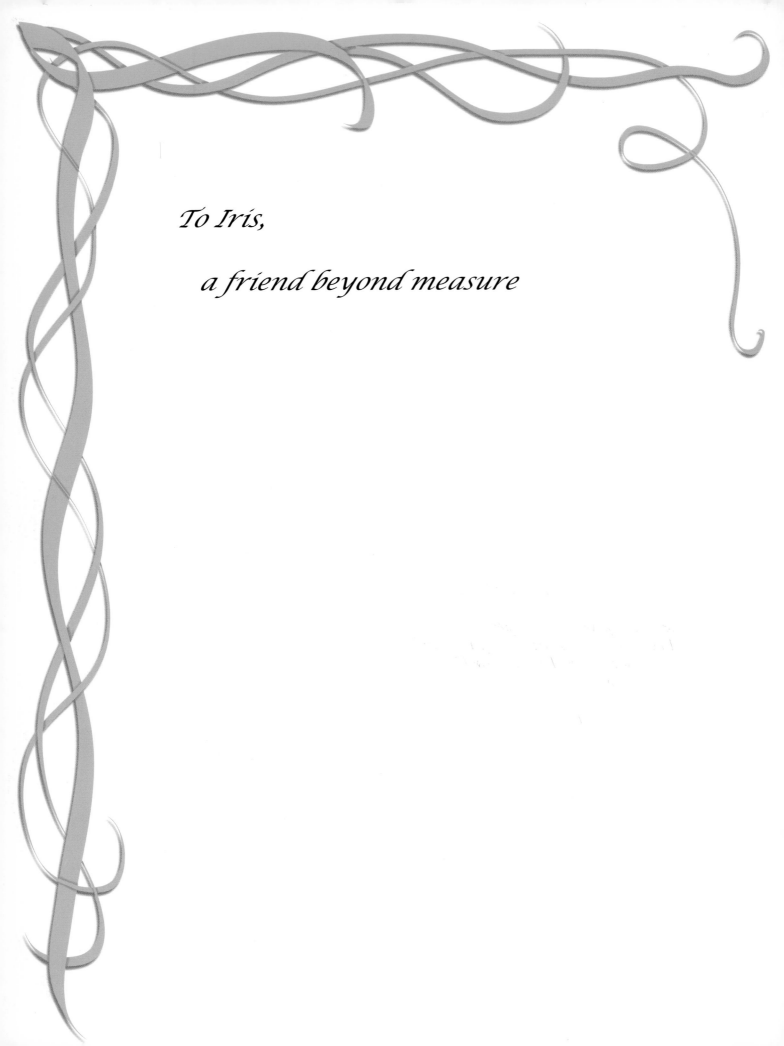

To Iris,

a friend beyond measure

I have so many people to thank for helping me write this book. Yes, indeed, I'm the Queen…of creative avoidance and procrastination! I'm richly blessed, however, to have a loving family and group of friends who made this book a reality. My dear friend, Iris Horton, lovingly got me off the starting mark and was a part of every page, photo, and recipe, even recruiting her sister to help. Iris, you were right when you said, "We're gonna birth this baby" —and you were the mid-wife. Through it all, Iris was my constant cheerleader and showed me a new meaning of friendship. I am forever grateful.

My husband, Kevin, patiently tolerated many late nights and a disrupted household and ate "photo-shoot" meals at inappropriate times and temperatures (usually cold), but was always available and quick to edit, do my bidding at the computer, and provided constant love, support, and encouragement. My daughter, Kelly, cheered me on from her home in Indonesia. My sister, Cherry Frye, spent many hours reading and revising, and was a wonderful sounding board for many decisions. Thank you, dear family, for loving me through it all.

My friend and former office assistant, Sarah Rutledge, coordinated our group of faithful recipe testers and got things organized in the early stages of the book. I appreciate Sarah's hard work and encouragement from start to finish, and I'm grateful for the time and care our testers devoted to this project.

Ralph Castellano, my wine guy and my friend, was quick to lend his expertise in recommending wines for each menu. We've had such fun over the years, teaching food and wine pairing classes, and swapping stories over many "sample glasses" of his merchandise. Thank you for your willingness to share your knowledge and for offering suggestions that make my meals taste even better!

I loved working with my photographer, Mike Bowlin! He was so committed to the project and was endlessly patient and accommodating as he worked around my crazy schedule. When my friends say the pictures make them hungry, I know I had the right guy for the job! Thank you so much, Mike; get ready for the next one!

I'm always amazed at the way God carefully places the right people in your path at the right time. I met my publishing consultant, Pam Van Scoyoc, in my neighborhood Kroger when she was selling her children's books. She and her son Ira, my graphic designer, have worked tirelessly to produce this cookbook. They remained cheerful as we've worked through many phases to find my "style." This book would never have been possible without your expert guidance and hard work. Thank you from the bottom of my heart!

Lastly I want to thank the cooking schools and culinary shops for inviting me to teach and share what I love. I so appreciate the beautiful venues and all the students who regularly attend my classes. It is truly music to my ears when I hear that my recipes were successfully made and presented to your friends and families. I hope you entertain often and make every day an occasion!

With heartfelt thanks to all,

Molly

Table of Contents

My Favorite Appetizers *6–17*

Prosciutto Palmiers - 9, Brie and Pear Quesadillas - 10, Blue Cheese Mousse - 11, Easy Dill Dip for Vegetable Crudités -12, Killer Chile con Queso - 13, Shrimp Dijon - 14, Spicy Party Nuts - 15, Bruschetta with Herbed Cheese and Tapenade – 16, 17

Brunch for Weekend Guests *18–33*

Mike's Drink - 21, Scotch Eggs with Dijon Sauce on Mixed Greens – 22, 23, Ricotta Tart with Leeks and Tomatoes – 24, 25, Green Beans with Herbed Crumb Topping – 26, 27, Banana Bread Pudding with Kahlúa Sauce – 28,29, Brunch Culinary Countdown – 30, 31, Brunch Shopping List – 32, 33

Elegant Dinner for Friends *34–47*

Salad of Pear, Roquefort, and Pecans on Mixed Greens with Celery Vinaigrette – 36, 37, Pan-Seared Salmon on Spinach with Wine-Shallot Sauce – 38, 39, Creamy Lemon Rice – 40, Oven-Roasted Asparagus – 41, Tropical Tart – 42, 43, Elegant Dinner Culinary Countdown – 44, 45, Elegant Dinner, Shopping List – 46, 47

Easy Italian *48–61*

Molly's Sensational Caesar Salad – 50, 51, Manicotti – 52, 53, Garlic-Sautéed Spinach – 54, Tony's Toast – 55, Tiramisu – 56, 57, Easy Italian Culinary Countdown – 58, 59, Easy Italian Shopping List – 60, 61

Sunday Family Dinner *62–75*

Salad with Greek Goddess Dressing – 64, 65, Perfect Roast Chicken with Gravy – 66, 67, Oven-Glazed Carrots – 67, Molly's Mashed Potatoes – 68, 69, Rosemary-Roasted New Potatoes – 68, Apple Pie in a Sack – 70, 71, Sunday Family Dinner Culinary Countdown – 72, 73, Sunday Family Dinner Shopping List – 74, 75

Autumn Company Dinner *76–89*

Butternut Bisque – 79, Apple and Romaine Salad – 80, Marinated Pork Tenderloin with Apricot Sauce – 82, Herb-Sautéed Vegetables – 84, Our Favorite Carrot Cake – 85, Autumn Company Dinner Culinary Countdown – 86, 87, Autumn Company Dinner Shopping List – 88, 89

My Best Tex-Mex *90–107*

Kevin's Margaritas – 93, Kevin's Roasted Salsa – 94, Roasted Corn Soup with Lime Cream – 96, South-of-the-Border Salad with Cumin Vinaigrette – 98, Green Chile Chicken Enchiladas – 101, Mexican Brownies – 102, Best Tex-Mex Culinary Countdown – 104, 105, Best Tex-Mex Shopping List – 106, 107

The Husband-Catching Supper *108–121*

Broccoli Salad – 111, Molly's Brisket – 112, Green Chile Rice – 114, Monte's Chocolate Sheath Cake – 117, Husband-Catching Supper Culinary Countdown – 118, 119, Husband-Catching Supper Shopping List – 120, 121

A Diva-licious Luncheon *122–137*

Shrimp Louis on Asparagus – 125, Curried Chicken and Artichoke Salad – 126, Salad of Roasted Beets and Panko-Crusted Goat Cheese with Lemon Vinaigrette – 128, Quick-Rise Dinner Rolls with Herbed Butter – 130, Elegant Chocolate Mousse with Raspberry Coulis – 132, 133, Diva-licious Luncheon Culinary Countdown – 134, 135, Diva-licious Luncheon Shopping List – 136, 137

Texas Cowhide Dinner *138–153*

Coconut Shrimp with Spicy Creole Dipping Sauce – 140, 141, Marinated Cucumber, Tomato, and Onion Salad – 142, Grilled Rib Roll with Spicy Peppercorn Sauce – 144, 145, Frizzled Onions – 143, Quick and Easy Horseradish Sauce – 146, Chipotle Corn Soufflé – 146, 147, Over-the-Top Tableside S'mores - 148, Chocolate Peanut Butter Pie – 149, Texas Cowhide Dinner Culinary Countdown – 150, 151, Texas Cowhide Dinner Shopping List – 152, 153

The Crowning Touch   A Dinner Fit for Royalty *154–171*

Smoked Salmon and Caviar Mousse – 156, 157, Boston Lettuce Salad in a Parmesan Bowl – 158, 159, Crown Roast of Pork with Fruited Stuffing – 160, 161, Layered Vegetable Soufflé – 164, 165, Hollandaise Sauce – 166, Orange Bowknot Rolls – 162, 163, Crème Brûlée with Raspberries – 167, Crowning Touch Culinary Countdown – 168, 169, Crowning Touch Shopping List – 170, 171

Index *172–173*

My Favorite Appetizers

Prosciutto Palmiers

Brie and Pear Quesadillas

Blue Cheese Mousse

Easy Dill Dip for Vegetable Crudités

Killer Chile con Queso

Shrimp Dijon

Spicy Party Nuts

Bruschetta with Herbed Cheese
and Tapenade

Unoaked Chardonnay
or Sancerre

Everyone I know is always looking for new recipe ideas for appetizers (I can't bear the thought of one more tortilla roll-up, can you?). These are some of my favorites; all are easy, delicious, and attractive presentations. Prepare one or two of them when you need that little something special to serve as friends gather for drinks before dinner. Remember, the purpose of the appetizer is to stimulate the palate, so something salty and savory does the trick. Cocktail time should be brief; forty-five minutes to one hour *max*! You want your guests to still have an appetite for the meal you're serving.

Keep things simple—not everything needs to be homemade. You can give store-bought items a personal touch with a fresh garnish or an interesting serving piece. Be sure to have plenty of appetizer plates and cocktail napkins, and position proper serving utensils for all the items. Try to anticipate the needs of your guests.

Please remember my foremost rule for entertaining~No matter how it turns out, it's absolutely perfect! Relax, enjoy your friends, and, most of all…be a guest at your own party!

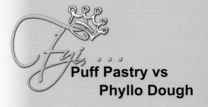

These are embarrassingly easy to prepare—and delicious. Perfect!

Prosciutto Palmiers

Makes 24 to 30

1 Pkg	**Puff pastry sheets, thawed**
	Spicy brown mustard
4 oz	**Thinly sliced prosciutto, about 10-12 slices**
¾ Cup	**Grated or shredded Parmesan cheese**

Preheat oven to 425°. Roll one sheet of pastry gently on a lightly floured surface to press out creases. Spread generously with mustard, sprinkle with half the cheese, and cover surface completely with prosciutto slices. Starting on one long side, roll tightly to the center in jelly-roll fashion. Roll the other long side to the center as well. Slice into 12-15 pieces, each ¼-½ inch wide, with a serrated knife and place on a parchment-lined baking sheet. Repeat with second sheet. Bake for 15-20 minutes or until golden brown. Serve hot.

Puff Pastry vs Phyllo Dough

Puff pastry and phyllo dough are two distinctly different pastry products and not used interchangeably. Both are found in the freezer section of the grocery store, and should be thawed slowly in the refrigerator (not at room temperature) before using. Puff pastry is made up of hundreds of layers of dough and butter. It is baked at a high temperature, usually 400° or more, which causes the moisture in the butter to create steam, thus creating puffy, thin, flaky layers. This type of pastry dough is used for croissants. Phyllo is tissue-thin sheets of pastry dough. Each layer is usually brushed with clarified butter, and multiple layers of phyllo dough are used in a dish. It dries out very quickly, so it is recommended that the bulk of the pastry be covered with a damp cloth while working with one sheet at a time. The dessert Baklava is made with phyllo dough.

Make-Ahead Tip: These can be formed into the rolls, sliced, left as a "log", tightly wrapped, and frozen. Remove from freezer, place on baking sheet, and bake from the frozen state, adding a few extra minutes to cooking time. They can also be made a day in advance, sliced and placed on the baking sheet, covered and refrigerated, and baked as needed for serving.

These quesadillas are open faced, not the type you normally get in a Mexican restaurant. You will impress your guests with these. The fruit and cheese offset the heat of the serrano beautifully, and this combination of flavors creates a party in your mouth!

Brie and Pear Quesadillas

Serves 8

4	**Flour tortillas**
¼ Medium	**Red onion, thinly sliced or minced**
2	**Pears, peel intact, sliced into thin lengthwise pieces**
1 (6-inch)	**Brie cheese round, sliced in thin slices** (I leave rind on)
2	**Fresh serrano chilies, minced** (or to taste)
	Kosher salt
	Minced fresh cilantro
4 Tbsp	**Cranberry chutney, or red jalapeno jelly or jam**

Fresh Serrano Chilies

Serrano chilies are small, slender, green peppers (you may also find red ones) with pointed tips. They are a bit hotter than jalapenos, but have a wonderful deep chile taste. If you desire less heat, substitute jalapenos.

Preheat the oven to 450°. Place tortillas directly on the oven rack or on a perforated or solid baking sheet. Bake tortillas in oven for 3-5 minutes. As they cook they may puff slightly. Place another baking sheet on top of them to weigh them down, and continue to cook until crisp. It is important that the tortillas be crisp before topping; otherwise, they will be soggy after the cheese melts.

Divide all the ingredients among the crisped tortillas, evenly spacing each item, starting with the red onion, then the pear slices, brie slices, and peppers, finishing with a sprinkle of salt. Place in the hot oven on a perforated baking sheet (if you have one) or a regular cookie sheet, and bake for 3-5 minutes or until the cheese melts. Remove from the oven and let rest for a couple of minutes, then cut each into 4 wedges so that a pear slice is on each wedge. Top with cilantro and a dollop of cranberry chutney. Serve hot.

Variation: This is also great with peaches or nectarines in place of pears, and blue cheese in place of brie.

Make-Ahead Tip: Crisp tortillas a day in advance and store in an airtight container. A few hours before serving, slice pears and submerge in lemon-lime soda to prevent browning. About an hour before serving, drain pears, and assemble the quesadillas. Refrigerate until time to bake and serve.

You always need a good spread in your repertoire of appetizer recipes, and this is the one to have. Amazingly, even people who are not fond of blue cheese like this savory spread. The Carr's Wheat Crackers are worth seeking out. You'll understand why when you taste them. Take a bite of cracker topped generously with the mousse, then a bite of apple...pure bliss!

Blue Cheese Mousse

Serves 20

1 Tbsp	**Unflavored gelatin**
¼ Cup	**Cold water**
12 oz	**Sour cream**
8 oz	**Cream cheese, softened**
1 Cup	**Small-curd cottage cheese** (not lowfat)
8 oz	**Good quality blue cheese, crumbled, at room temperature**
2 Tbsp	**Minced fresh chives**
¾ tsp	**Dried oregano**
½ tsp	**Garlic powder**
½ tsp	**Onion powder**
½ tsp	**Hot pepper sauce**
	Carr's Wheat Crackers (or other sweet wheat crackers) **to serve**
	Apples, grapes, and candied walnuts (optional)

Sprinkle gelatin over water. Allow to "bloom" (a process in which the gelatin granules swell) for about 5 minutes. Transfer to a small saucepan. Over low heat, stir until dissolved. Set aside, but do not allow to set; rewarm if necessary. Combine sour cream, cream cheese, cottage cheese, and blue cheese in food processor. Process until smooth. Add chives, seasonings, hot sauce, and dissolved gelatin mixture. Blend well.

Grease a 4-cup mold with no-stick cooking spray. Line with plastic wrap, using enough to extend over the sides of the mold; smooth out wrinkles and spray again. Fill with blue cheese mixture and lightly tap on counter to help settle. Refrigerate for 4 hours or overnight to set. Unmold onto lettuce-lined plate, using the plastic wrap to help ease the mixture from the mold. Garnish with sliced apples, grapes, and/or candied walnuts. Best served with Carr's Wheat Crackers.

This recipe was a catering standby of mine, and I still make it for every cocktail party. I find it amusing when guests think that eating raw vegetables offsets the calorie-laden drinks and desserts~Ha! Think beyond the usual platter of veggies in a circle with dip in the center; present individual servings instead. Place dip in the bottom of small cups; stand vegetables upright. This also eliminates the worry of the "double dipper" at the veggie platter.

Easy Dill Dip for Vegetable Crudites

Makes about 1½ Cups

1 Cup	**Mayonnaise** *(light or regular)*
1/3 Cup	**Sour cream** *(light or regular)*
1 Tbsp	**Lemon zest**
1 Tbsp	**Lemon juice**
4	**Green onions, thinly sliced, including tops**
1 tsp	**Beau Monde seasoning** *(made by Spice Island)*
3 Tbsp	**Minced fresh dill** *(or 1 Tbsp dried dill weed)*
Dash	**Hot sauce**

Mix together all ingredients and chill. Flavors improve overnight. Serve with raw vegetables, on baked potatoes, or over grilled fish or chicken.

Please slice your vegetables yourself. The store-bought veggie trays are tacky (sorry, but it's the truth).

Make-Ahead Tip: Prepare the dip one or two days in advance. Refrigerate until serving.

The beauty of this queso is that it is a low-stress item. Because it doesn't congeal into a solid mass when it cools, you're not constantly worried about keeping it piping hot! It is a "must-have" at our family gatherings, and also makes a super-yummy sauce for enchiladas!

"Killer" Chile con Queso

Serves 10-12

1 (10¾-oz) Can	**Cream of chicken soup, undiluted**
¾ Cup	**Evaporated milk**
1 (7-oz) Can	**Diced green chilies**
2 Tbsp	**Minced jalapenos** (optional)
1 (4-oz) Jar	**Chopped pimiento, drained**
1 tsp	**Ground cumin**
1 (1-oz) Pkg	**Ranch dip mix**
1 Can	**Rotel Tomatoes and Peppers**
1 lb	**Processed cheese food** (I use Velveeta), **cut into cubes**
¼ Cup	**Minced fresh cilantro**
	Minced fresh cilantro for garnish
	Tortilla chips for dipping

Combine soup, evaporated milk, green chilies, jalapenos, pimiento, cumin, dip mix, and Rotel in a medium saucepan. Cook over low heat, stirring frequently. When bubbly, add cheese and cilantro, and stir until cheese melts and mixture is combined. Be sure to keep the heat low, and stir constantly after adding the cheese to prevent scorching. Serve warm with tortilla chips, reheating as needed.

Make-Ahead Tip: This queso can be made ahead or even frozen and reheated before your event. I prefer to reheat it in the microwave.

How To ...
Cook Shrimp

To my mind, the worst thing you can do is overcook shrimp!

Here's how I do it: bring a large pot of water to a rolling boil. Add salt and any seasonings you like (crab or shrimp boil, celery, peppercorns, lemon slices, etc.). Add shrimp (shell-on gives better flavor) and stir. As soon as you see the majority of the shrimp turn opaque and begin to curl, take the pot off the heat. Drain in a colander and immediately cover the shrimp with ice to stop the cooking. Timing varies depending on the amount of shrimp, how cold they are, and so on. Peel when cool.

Hopefully, there are some of you who don't already have this recipe—I've given it out so many times over the years! Talk about easy! This goes together in a snap and everyone adores it. Use nice large shrimp, tails on, to make it pretty, and easy to eat.

Shrimp Dijon

Serves 20

Marinade:

¼ Cup	**Finely minced fresh Italian flat-leaf parsley**
¼ Cup	**Finely chopped shallots** *(not green onions!!)*
¼ Cup	**Tarragon vinegar**
¼ Cup	**White wine vinegar**
4 Tbsp	**Dijon mustard**
2 tsp	**Crushed red pepper** *(use less if you don't like it spicy)*
2 tsp	**Salt**
	Freshly ground black pepper
½ Cup	**Extra-virgin olive oil**
2½ lbs	**Large shrimp, cooked, peeled, leaving tail on, and deveined**

To prepare the marinade: Place parsley, shallots, vinegars, mustard, red pepper, salt, and pepper in the bowl of a food processor. Pulse first to chop everything evenly, then purée. While the machine is running, add the oil in a slow stream.

Pour over the shrimp and toss gently. Transfer to a zip-top bag. Refrigerate and marinate several hours or overnight for best flavor. Drain marinade and discard. Serve shrimp alone or with canapé toasts as an appetizer, or on leaf lettuce as an elegant first course!

I know many of you are thinking, "Is she nuts? Marinate shrimp with all that vinegar overnight? It will make a mushy mess!" I don't know *why* it doesn't...it just doesn't. It's delicious; I promise.

Make-Ahead Tip: Prepare a day in advance and allow to marinate overnight.

Nice salty nuts make great snacks with cocktails. These are positively addictive. They also make a nice hostess gift—simply package in a cellophane bag and tie with colorful ribbon.

Spicy Party Nuts

Makes 4 Cups

4 Cups	**Mixed nuts** *(whole almonds, pecan halves, cashews)*
1	**Egg white**
4 tsp	**Dark brown sugar**
2 tsp	**Salt** *(a bit less if using salted nuts)*
½ tsp	**Cayenne pepper**
2 Tbsp	**Finely minced fresh rosemary**

Spread nuts on an ungreased baking sheet and bake for 10-15 minutes at 325º, stirring occasionally. Remove from oven; cool slightly. Beat egg white until frothy. Add sugar, salt, cayenne, and rosemary. Blend. Stir in nuts and coat well. Place nuts back on baking sheet and return to the oven. Bake for 15-20 minutes or until golden. Cool and store in an airtight container. Yummy!

Make-Ahead Tip: These can be made several days in advance of your party.

These bruschetta show off the colors of the Italian flag and are as delicious as they are beautiful. In one bite, you're magically transported to one of my favorite places in the world!

Bruschetta with Herbed Cheese and Tapenade

Serves 20

Bruschetta:
2	**Baguettes**
½ Cup	**Olive oil**
	Dried Italian Herb Seasoning

Herbed Cheese Topping:
4 oz	**Feta cheese**
8 oz	**Cream cheese, softened**
1 clove	**Garlic, pressed**
1½ tsp	**Minced fresh oregano** *(or ¾ tsp dried oregano)*
2 tsp	**Minced fresh basil** *(or ½ tsp dried basil)*
2 or 3 Tbsp	**Milk** *(2% or whole),* **if needed to get spreadable consistency**

Tapenade:
½ Cup	**Minced sun-dried, oil-packed tomatoes, drained**
½ Cup	**Small pitted kalamata olives**
¼ Cup	**Minced fresh basil**
	Fresh basil leaves or parsley for garnish

For the Bruschetta: Thinly slice baguettes on the diagonal. Brush one side with olive oil and sprinkle with Italian herbs. Place on baking sheet and toast under broiler. Turn and repeat on other side. Remove to rack to cool.

For the Herbed Cheese Topping: In the bowl of a food processor, combine feta cheese, cream cheese, garlic, oregano, and basil. Blend well. Add milk to get desired spreading consistency. Remove to a separate bowl.

For the Tapenade: In the bowl of a food processor, combine sun-dried tomatoes, olives, and fresh basil. Process with quick pulses until well blended.

To assemble: Spread generous amount of cheese topping on toasted baguette slices. Top with a bit of the tapenade. Garnish with a fresh basil leaf or a sprig of fresh parsley.

Make-Ahead Tip: The bruschetta, topping, and tapenade can all be made a day in advance. Assemble a few hours before serving. Cover and refrigerate.

Brunch for Weekend Guests

Mike's Drink

Scotch Eggs with Dijon Sauce
on Mixed Greens

Ricotta Tart
with Leeks and Tomatoes

Green Beans
with Herbed Crumb Topping

Banana Bread Pudding
with Kahlúa Sauce

Champagne

Preparing meals for weekend houseguests can be great fun—but when the menu is too complicated, you're likely to find an extra helping of stress along with the food. Since I believe in stress-free entertaining, this combination of dishes is ideal. This brunch menu is a perfect way to show your guests they are loved and very special. These recipes are delicious, colorful, and a little out of the ordinary—and whether you prepare one or all, you'll find they will be met with rave reviews. And while you're at it, you'll also see how beautiful a presentation can be… because food should look as great as it tastes!

As my guests gather, we begin with a festive champagne cocktail. The Scotch Eggs are, admittedly, a pain in the neck to make, but oh so yummy. But, take heart, this is the only recipe of the bunch that is time consuming—the rest are a snap to prepare! Just let your guests know you only make them for *very* special people. The Ricotta Tart is not as custard-like as a quiche, and perfectly complements the eggs. And then there is dessert…Oh Baby, Oh Baby! This one is over the top! What makes this bread pudding different is that the bread is torn, not cut. This leaves a very coarse and rough top that gets nice and crispy. The pudding is put into the oven immediately after pouring on the cream mixture, so it doesn't get heavy and soggy. And then, there's the sauce. To quote a dear friend of mine, Judy, "Sauce is a beverage. It should be poured into a cup and enjoyed in a room all by yourself." You'll see what I mean. It is scrumptious. Enjoy treating your guests to this memorable meal.

I love to set the mood for any special occasion with a fun cocktail. This one is especially meaningful to me. When I lived in Denver and was newly single, I had the greatest neighbor, Mike. What a guy!!! He was always such fun, loved to cook, and had a wicked sense of humor. He called once and asked if I'd like a fresh apricot pie. Of course, who wouldn't? As I waited in anticipation, the doorbell rang. There was Mike with a pie plate—and a sack of apricots. He said, "Call me when it's ready!!!" *I* got to make the pie for the two of us to enjoy!

Very sadly, Mike became ill—but he had planned every detail of his memorial celebration, down to the food and drink. He wanted his favorite (and very potent) cocktail served, with the wish that his friends would celebrate so much the cops would have to come and break up the party! Fortunately, I left before they did!

I'm happy to share this recipe with you. It always brings a smile to my face as I remember a friend who had a real zest for living! Cheers!

This cocktail is only as good as its components. I use Chambord, though pricey, because it has a beautiful deep garnet-red color, and nice viscosity. There are less expensive liqueurs of similar flavor, but I can't guarantee the drink will be as beautiful. Don't buy an inexpensive vodka or cheap sparkling wine—result: BIG headache!

Cooking with Wines, Liqueurs, and Spirits

Always cook with something you would be willing to drink. This means no "cooking wines", and not wine that you left out on the counter several days ago. If it is not good enough for you to drink a glass of it, it will not magically transform into something better because you cook it! White zinfandel doesn't qualify under any circumstance!!! Keep in mind, liqueurs and spirits have higher alcohol contents than wine, making them highly flammable. Do not pour directly from the bottle into the pan. It is always best to slightly warm the measured liqueur first, turn off the burner, then add the liqueur, and ignite with a long match.

Mike's Drink

One cocktail

½ oz	**Chilled Chambord**
	(or other black raspberry liqueur)
1 oz	**Chilled vodka**
	Chilled dry champagne
	Fresh raspberries to garnish

Pour the raspberry liqueur into a champagne flute. Slowly pour vodka down the side of the glass. Fill with champagne. Garnish with a few raspberries if desired.

Enjoy, and celebrate the day!

Make-Ahead Tip: Chill all ingredients two days ahead. Wash raspberries the morning of the brunch; gently spin in a salad spinner to dry. Return berries to refrigerator until serving time.

Hard-Cook an Egg

Here's a burning question that has plagued cooks forever: "How do you hard-cook an egg and have it easy to peel, with no ugly gray-green ring around the yolk?"

The eggs will peel best if they are 1-2 weeks old. The discoloration around the yolk occurs less often in fresh eggs and in eggs not cooked at excessively high temperatures. This means you must plan in advance and buy your eggs about a week before you cook them. This is just about the right time frame for the egg to peel easily but still be fresh enough not to get the ring around the yolk.

OK…here's what I do. Place eggs in a saucepan in a single layer, without crowding, and cover with cold water. Place the saucepan on the stove and heat, uncovered, over medium-high heat until the water *just* begins to boil. Immediately turn down the heat to a very gentle simmer and continue to cook uncovered for 9 minutes. Drain at once and plunge the eggs into ice water until cool enough to handle.

Scotch Eggs with Dijon Sauce on Mixed Greens

Serves 6

Eggs:

6 Large	Eggs, hard-cooked and peeled
	All-purpose flour for dredging
1 lb	Bulk spicy breakfast sausage
2 Large	Eggs, beaten
2 Cups	Seasoned dry bread crumbs
	Oil for deep-frying *(I usually use canola)*
4 Cups	Mixed spring greens

To prepare the eggs: Dredge peeled eggs in flour to coat. Divide sausage into 6 equal portions and pat out each into 4-inch circle. Mold each sausage portion around an egg to encase it completely. Dip sausage-covered eggs in beaten egg, then roll in the dry bread crumbs to coat. Place on a baking sheet and refrigerate 30 minutes. Heat oil *(a depth of 3 inches)* to 375° in a saucepan or deep skillet. Deep-fry a few eggs at a time until dark golden brown and sausage is cooked through. Drain eggs on a rack over paper towels. When cool enough to handle, slice eggs in half, lengthwise, place on top of greens, and drizzle with the Dijon sauce. The eggs may be served warm or at room temperature.

Make-Ahead Tip: Fry eggs the day before, but do not slice. After cooling to room temperature, refrigerate until completely chilled, then cover. The morning of the brunch, remove eggs from the refrigerator about 45 minutes before serving time. Warm eggs on a baking sheet in a 300° oven for 15 minutes. Slice, place on greens, and drizzle with sauce. Prepare the sauce a day or two in advance.

Dijon Sauce:

½ Cup	*Sour cream*
½ Cup	*Mayonnaise*
⅓ Cup	*Whole grain Dijon mustard*

To prepare the Dijon Sauce: Stir together the sour cream, mayonnaise, and whole grain mustard. Chill until serving time.

This tart is better than a quiche—not quite so eggy. It makes a nice light luncheon dish as well!

Ricotta Tart with Leeks and Tomatoes

Serves 8

1 (9")	**Pie crust** *(rolled type in refrigerated section is preferred)*
1	**Leek, thinly sliced** *(white and pale green parts only)*
2 Tbsp	**Unsalted utter**
1¼ Cups	**Ricotta cheese**
2 Large	**Eggs, beaten**
¼ Cup	**Heavy whipping cream**
¼ Cup	**Grated Parmesan cheese**
1 Tbsp	**Fresh thyme leaves** *(or 1 tsp dried thyme)*
1 Tbsp	**Minced fresh Italian flat-leaf parsley or basil**
	Salt and freshly ground white pepper to taste
2-3 Medium	**Ripe Roma tomatoes, thinly sliced**
	Additional grated Parmesan cheese
	Additional minced Italian flat-leaf parsley or basil to garnish

Preheat oven to 350°. Line a 9-inch pie plate with the crust and flute the edges. You may use a 9-inch removable-bottom tart pan if you prefer.

In a small skillet, sauté the leek in butter until tender (about 3 minutes). Set aside to cool slightly. In a medium bowl, stir together the remaining ingredients except tomatoes. Add leeks and any remaining butter in the pan. Spread into the crust, top with the sliced tomatoes, and sprinkle with additional cheese. Bake 40-50 minutes or until the tart is golden and set. Garnish each slice with additional minced parsley or basil. Serve warm or cold.

Make-Ahead Tip: The day before, line pan with pie crust, cover, and refrigerate. Prepare the leek and ricotta filling and refrigerate. About an hour before serving, fill crust, top with tomatoes, and bake.

How To ...
Buy and Prepare Leeks

Leeks are related to garlic and onions and look like giant scallions *(green onions)*. They have a mild taste and are used often in European kitchens. Their dark green leaves are tough and fibrous, so use only the white and pale green parts of the base or bulb. The leek's growth habit often traps dirt between its layers. Slice leeks in half lengthwise and rinse thoroughly to remove all the grit. Use in cooking as you would an onion.

Green Beans with Herbed Crumb Topping

Serves 6-8

How To . . .
Make Soft, Fresh Bread Crumbs

Remove the crust from a loaf of sturdy bread—like French or Italian. You want bread that has a firm texture, NOT "gloppy sandwich bread," as my mom would say (you know, that soft, squishy bread that sticks to the roof of your mouth!). Tear the bread into small pieces and place in the bowl of a food processor. It's best to do this in small batches. Pulse until you get uniform crumbs. Any unused crumbs can be frozen in a zip-top bag.

Crumbs:

6 Tbsp	Unsalted butter
1 Clove	Garlic, pressed
2 Tbsp	Italian flat-leaf parsley, minced
2 Tbsp	Sliced chives
1¾ Cups	Soft, fresh bread crumbs
1 Tbsp	Lemon zest
	Salt and pepper

Green Beans:

2 lbs	Whole green beans, cooked tender-crisp

To prepare the crumbs: Melt the butter in a large skillet or sauté pan over medium-high heat. Stir in garlic, parsley, chives, bread crumbs, lemon zest, and salt and pepper. Cook over medium heat, stirring often, until the crumbs are crisp and golden.

To serve: Spoon hot crumb mixture over hot cooked green beans and serve at once.

Variation: Substitute fresh asparagus for the green beans.

Make-Ahead Tip: The day before, cook beans tender-crisp. Plunge into ice water to stop the cooking. Drain, pat dry, and refrigerate. An hour before serving, remove beans from refrigerator. Prepare the bread crumb mixture. Set skillet aside on stovetop. When ready to serve, heat bread crumbs, add green beans, and stir to warm through.

Since brunch is usually served late in the morning (or closer to lunch than to breakfast), there is always the dilemma of what side dishes to serve. I like to include some sort of green vegetable. It adds bright color to the plate and is sort of a transitional component to bridge the gap between breakfast foods and lunch foods. This green bean dish, with its crisp topping, is easy to prepare and complements the creamy tart.

Toast Nuts

Place nuts in a nonstick skillet over medium heat. Do not add oil or butter. The heat brings out the natural oil from the nuts so they will not stick. Stir until the nuts become aromatic and begin to color. Do not walk away! They can burn in an instant! Remove from the heat and from the skillet to stop cooking! Nuts can also be toasted on an ungreased baking sheet in a 325° oven for about 10 minutes. Stir and check often to be sure they do not get too dark.

Banana Bread Pudding

Serves 12

Pudding:

1 Large	Loaf French bread, crust on, torn up (not sliced)
2	Ripe (but firm) bananas, thinly sliced
⅔ Cup	Raisins (optional)
6	Eggs, beaten
2	Ripe bananas, mashed
4 Cups	Half & Half
1½ Cups	Sugar
1 tsp	Ground cinnamon
½ tsp	Salt
1 Tbsp	Pure vanilla extract

Topping:

6 Tbsp	Unsalted butter, melted
6 Tbsp	Dark brown sugar
½ Cup	Finely chopped toasted pecans
	Kahlúa Sauce (recipe follows)
	Whipped cream (to garnish)
	Ground cinnamon (to garnish)
	Chopped pecans (to garnish)

To prepare the pudding: Preheat oven to 350°. Butter a 9 x 13-inch baking dish. Lightly mix together the torn bread, sliced bananas, and raisins, and place in the prepared baking dish. In a large bowl combine the eggs, mashed bananas, Half & Half, sugar, cinnamon, salt, and vanilla. Pour over the bread. Immediately place in the preheated oven. You do not want the bread to get totally saturated with the egg mixture. This is what gives this bread pudding its nice, light texture! Bake, uncovered, for 1 hour. Remove from oven.

To prepare the topping: Drizzle top of baked pudding with melted butter and sprinkle with brown sugar and pecans. Put back into oven for 5-10 minutes, until brown sugar is bubbly and nuts are lightly toasted. Remove and cool slightly before serving.

Make-Ahead Tip: The bread pudding can be completely baked the day before, but if you choose to do this, do not top with the brown sugar, butter, and pecans. Refrigerate after baking. About an hour before serving, remove the bread pudding from the refrigerator and allow to come almost to room temperature. Top with the butter, brown sugar, and nuts and heat, uncovered, in a 350° oven 15-20 minutes.

Just to confess, we always double the sauce. It's just so, so good!! Any leftover sauce is great on ice cream, pound cake, or eaten directly from a spoon while standing in front of the open fridge! You'll see!

Kahlúa Sauce

Serves 12

1½ Cups	**Sugar**
1 (5.33-oz) Can	**Evaporated milk** *(not sweetened condensed milk!!)*
4 Tbsp	**Unsalted butter, melted**
1 Large	**Egg, beaten**
1 Tsp	**Pure vanilla extract**
¼ Cup	**Kahlúa** *(or other coffee-flavored liqueur)* **or bourbon whiskey**

In a medium saucepan, before placing over heat, stir together the sugar, evaporated milk, butter, and eggs. Stir to blend thoroughly. Place pan over medium-low heat; cook and stir constantly. Mixture will begin to boil and thicken, and sugar will dissolve completely. Remove from heat and add vanilla and liqueur. Stir well. Strain sauce through a fine-mesh sieve if desired. Chill sauce until serving time.

Serve bread pudding warm with cold sauce and top with a dollop of whipped cream, a sprinkle of cinnamon, and a few chopped pecans scattered over the top.

Listen for the moans!!! Oh baby, oh baby!

Make-Ahead Tip: Prepare sauce two days ahead and keep refrigerated until serving time. Please note: there is no need to check the quality of the sauce. If you do, there will probably not be enough left for the guests! It is REALLY yummy. After all…it's all about the sauce!

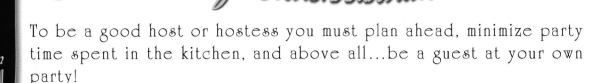

Culinary Countdown

To be a good host or hostess you must plan ahead, minimize party time spent in the kitchen, and above all...be a guest at your own party!

4 Days Before: Follow up on RSVPs; verify number of guests.

3 Days Before: Gather and make ready all table linens, dishes, flatware, glasses, serving utensils, and salt and pepper grinders; plan or order centerpiece; decide on additional beverages.

2 Days Before: Edit grocery list; shop for all items, including wines, spirits, and liqueurs.

Chill all components for the cocktail.

Set the table—completely!

Cook and peel eggs for Scotch Eggs; make Dijon Sauce.

Make Kahlúa sauce for bread pudding.

1 Day Before: Encase eggs in sausage, roll in crumbs, refrigerate, then fry. Refrigerate the eggs, covering after they are completely chilled. Wash salad greens.

Line tart pan with crust; cover, and refrigerate. Prepare filling; refrigerate.

Cook beans tender-crisp and chill, or place frozen beans in the refrigerator to thaw. Make soft bread crumbs and store them in a zip-top bag. Chop and zest lemons for the topping; refrigerate.

Prepare and bake bread pudding, but do not add topping. Chill. Chop and toast pecans for topping and garnish.

Party Day: **Relax!!**

1½ Hours Before: Wash raspberries for cocktails, refrigerate until serving.

Remove Scotch Eggs, tart crust and filling, green beans, and bread pudding from the refrigerator. Preheat oven(s).

Whip cream for dessert and place in sieve in refrigerator.

1 Hour Before: Fill tart shell; top with tomatoes and cheese; bake.

Make crumb mixture for green beans and set aside.

30 Minutes Before: Set out cocktail ingredients; keep chilled if possible.

Put topping on bread pudding and put in oven to warm.

Warm Scotch Eggs in oven, remove, slice, and plate.

Slice tart and plate.

Serve bread pudding leisurely.

Savor the Moment!

Brunch for Weekend Guests

For 6 people

Produce

- [ ] 4 — Ripe *(but firm)* bananas
- [ ] 1 Small box — Fresh raspberries
- [ ] 1 Large — Lemon
- [ ] 2 lbs — Fresh whole green beans
- [ ] 1 Large — Leek
- [ ] 2 Tbsp — Fresh chives
- [ ] 2-3 Medium — Ripe Roma tomatoes
- [ ] 4 Cups — Mixed spring greens
- [ ] 1 Clove — Garlic
- [ ] 5 Tbsp — Fresh minced Italian flat-leaf parsley or basil
- [ ] 1 Tbsp — Fresh minced thyme

Dairy & Eggs

- [ ] 2¼ Cups — Unsalted butter
- [ ] 4 Cups — Half & Half
- [ ] 2¼ Cups — Heavy whipping cream
- [ ] ½ Cup — Sour cream
- [ ] 17 large — Eggs

Cheese & Deli

- [ ] ½ Cup — Grated Parmesan cheese
- [ ] 1¼ Cups — Ricotta cheese

Meat & Fish

- [ ] 1 lb — Bulk spicy breakfast sausage

Canned Vegetables, Fruits, & Dried Fruits

- [ ] 2/3 Cup — Raisins *(optional in Bread Pudding)*

Baking, Spices, & Nuts

- [ ] 3 Cups — Sugar
- [ ] 6 Tbsp — Dark brown sugar

☐	1 Cup	All-purpose flour
☐	4 tsp	Pure vanilla extract
☐	2 Cups	Seasoned dry bread crumbs
☐	1 tsp	Ground cinnamon
☐	1 Cup	Chopped pecans
☐	1 (5.33-oz) Can	Evaporated milk

Condiments

☐	48 oz	Oil for deep frying *(I use canola oil)*
☐	½ Cup	Mayonnaise
☐	⅓ Cup	Whole grain Dijon mustard

Breads

☐	1 (9")	Pie crust *(the rolled type in refrigerated section is preferred)*
☐	1¾ Cups	Fresh, soft bread crumbs *(from French- or Italian-type bread)*
☐	1 Lg. Loaf	French bread

Wine & Spirits

☐	4 oz	Chambord *(or other black raspberry liqueur)* for 8 cocktails
☐	8 oz	Vodka for 8 cocktails
☐	32 oz	Dry champagne or Sparkling wine for 8 cocktails
☐	¼ Cup	Kahlúa *(or other coffee-flavored liqueur)* or bourbon whiskey
☐		Champagne *(recommended wine for meal)*

Elegant Dinner for Friends

Salad of Pear, Roquefort, and Pecans on Mixed Greens with Celery Vinaigrette

Pan-Seared Salmon on Spinach with Wine-Shallot Sauce

Creamy Lemon Rice

Oven-Roasted Asparagus

Tropical Tart

Full-Bodied Chardonnay

If ever there were the perfect company meal, this is it! It's so easy to prepare, and always well received by guests. This is my most requested salad. As a good Texas girl, I love it with pecans, but it is delicious with walnuts or cashews. It can be turned into a main-dish salad with the addition of cooked, diced chicken! In the event you have a guest who does not like fish, this entrée is great with chicken breast instead (be sure to pound the boneless, skinless chicken breast to an even thickness to ensure quick, even cooking). The beauty of this menu is that much can be made ahead, allowing you to spend more time with your guests.

When planning a meal, it is important to keep in mind the colors, flavors, and textures of the foods on the plate. No matter how fabulous the tastes may be, if everything on the plate is the same color and texture, it will not be a great meal! We feast first with the eye then with the palate, so the presentation on each plate needs to be visually appealing. The arrangement on the plate and the combination of the colors can influence our overall impression of the dinner. Also, when setting the table, try to use unscented candles (or very faintly scented ones) when at all possible. Avoid floral centerpieces that have strongly scented flowers. They, too, can be very distracting to your taste buds. For this dinner, you'll want your guests to savor every bite!

You may receive applause after your guests taste this salad~take a bow!

Salad of Pears, Roquefort, and Pecans on Mixed Greens with Celery Vinaigrette

Serves 6-8

Pecans:

1½ Cups	Pecans (halves or coarsely chopped)
2 Tbsp	Unsalted butter, melted
2 tsp	Sugar
Dash	Cayenne pepper (optional)
	Salt and pepper to taste

Salad:

2	Ripe, (but firm), pears, thinly sliced (I use red pears, peel left on)
8 oz	Roquefort cheese, crumbled
2 Tbsp	Fresh minced tarragon or Italian flat-leaf parsley for garnish
6-8 Cups	Mixed greens for salad

Vinaigrette:

¼ Cup	Sugar
⅓ Cup	Apple cider vinegar
1 tsp	Dry mustard
1 Clove	Garlic, minced
	Salt and pepper to taste
1 Small stalk	Celery, chopped
Dash	Hot sauce
1 Cup	Canola oil (or light olive oil or grape seed oil)

To prepare the pecans: Preheat oven to 350°. In a bowl, combine pecans, butter, sugar, cayenne, salt, and pepper. Stir until nuts are coated. Spread out on a baking sheet and bake for 10-12 minutes or until lightly browned. Set aside to cool.

To prepare the salad: Arrange salad greens on a large platter. Top with pears, cheese, and pecans. Drizzle with vinaigrette. Sprinkle with tarragon or parsley.

To prepare the vinaigrette: Place all ingredients **except oil** in the bowl of a food processor or in a blender. Process until combined and celery is puréed. With machine running, add oil in a slow, steady stream. Blend until emulsified. Refrigerate until serving. If dressing separates, shake well or reprocess in food processor. Store any remaining dressing in refrigerator for up to one week.

Variations: Try other types of nuts. Walnuts, almonds, or cashews are delicious. If you are not a fan of the strong taste of Roquefort, a milder blue-veined cheese will do (perhaps a young Gorgonzola). Feta is also yummy in this salad. Depending on availability, try apples or peaches instead of pears. Feel free to give it your own "magic" touch!

Make-Ahead Tip: Prepare nuts a day or two in advance; store in a zip-top bag at room temperature. Make the vinaigrette a day in advance, store in a squeeze bottle in the refrigerator. Wash salad greens a day ahead. Early on the day of the event, slice pears and cover with lemon-lime soda to prevent browning. Refrigerate and drain before using.

Shallots

First and foremost—shallots are NOT green onions! (Those are scallions!) Shallots are formed more like garlic than onions, growing in large cloves. They have a papery skin, usually brown or reddish brown, and whitish flesh tinged with purple. A medium size is about the size of a walnut shell; large is about the size of a ping-pong ball. They have a mild onion flavor with a slight garlic overtone, making them ideal for delicately flavored dishes, where onion would overpower.

Pan-Seared Salmon on Spinach with Wine-Shallot Sauce

Serves 6

Salmon:

6 (4-oz)	**Salmon fillets, skinless preferred**
	Salt and pepper
2 Tbsp	**Olive oil**
1 Tbsp	**Unsalted butter**

Wilted Spinach:

	Additional olive oil if needed
2 Large	**Shallots, thinly sliced**
2 Tbsp	**Minced fresh tarragon** *(or 2 tsp dried tarragon)*
1½ -2 lbs	**Fresh baby spinach, washed and spun dry**

Wine-Shallot Sauce:

2 Tbsp	**Olive oil**
2 Tbsp	**Unsalted butter**
2 Large	**Shallots, thinly sliced**
8 oz	**Sliced button mushrooms**
2 Tbsp	**Minced fresh tarragon** *(or 2 tsp dried tarragon)*
1 Cup	**Champagne or dry white wine**
¾ Cup	**Whipping cream**
	Salt and pepper to taste

To prepare the salmon: Season salmon with salt and pepper. Heat 2 Tbsp olive oil and 1 Tbsp butter in a large nonstick skillet over medium-high heat. Add salmon, presentation side down *(or skin side up)*, taking care not to crowd the pan. *Depending on the size of your pan, you may need to cook salmon in two batches.* Sauté until golden brown, about 2-3 minutes, turn, and continue to cook until done, about 3-4 minutes longer. Remove salmon to a platter. Cover and keep warm, reserving the skillet for the spinach.

To prepare the spinach: A few minutes before serving, prepare the spinach. Heat the same skillet used for the salmon over medium-high heat, adding more olive oil if necessary. *There should be a light coating of oil covering the bottom of the pan.* Sauté half the shallots and tarragon for about one minute or until the shallots are translucent. Add spinach, and turn with tongs just until wilted.

To prepare the sauce: In another skillet, NOT nonstick, heat the olive oil and butter over medium-high heat. Add shallots, mushrooms, and tarragon, and sauté until mushrooms begin to brown. While stirring, add wine to deglaze the pan, and simmer uncovered until reduced by half. Add cream, taste for seasonings, and simmer until slightly thickened. To serve, mound spinach on plate, top with fish, and ladle sauce on top.

Variation: Substitute boneless, skinless chicken breasts for the salmon. Pound to an even thickness between sheets of plastic wrap. Prepare like the salmon, but if browned ahead, bake in oven 12-15 minutes to cook through.

Make-Ahead Tip: Make sauce the day before. Reheat in microwave or on the stovetop before serving. Early in the day, brown the salmon on both sides in the nonstick skillet, transfer to a sheet pan, and refrigerate. Remove about 30 minutes before serving time. Let rest 20 minutes at room temperature, then bake uncovered at 350° for 8-10 minutes.

This is rice like you've never tasted before! It is creamy like a risotto, but much easier to prepare, and is the perfect companion to fish (or lamb!), with its intense lemon flavor and fresh herbs. My daughter, Kelly, aka the "Golden Child," once said, "White rice is a waste of time in my mouth." She changed her mind when she tasted this recipe!

Creamy Lemon Rice

Serves 6

4 Tbsp	**Unsalted butter**
1 Cup	**Long grain rice**
	Zest (grated peel) **of one large lemon**
2 Cups	**Chicken broth, boiling**
1 tsp	**Salt**
2 Tbsp	**Lemon juice**
½ Cup	**Whipping cream** (or more if desired)**, heated**
2 Tbsp	**Minced fresh herbs** (parsley, dill, tarragon, basil, or a combination)

Melt butter in a medium saucepan. Add rice and lemon zest, stir to coat. Cook, stirring often, over medium heat for about 5 minutes. The rice grains will become opaque, but not browned. Add hot broth and salt. *Why hot broth? It doesn't cool down the pot, which would increase the cooking time.* Reduce heat, cover, and simmer for about 20 minutes until liquid is absorbed. Stir in lemon juice and heated cream. Increase heat slightly and stir until most of the cream has been absorbed. Stir in fresh herbs. Serve immediately.

Make-Ahead Tip: A day ahead, prepare the rice with the lemon zest, broth, and salt as directed. Cool, put into a microwave-safe container, and refrigerate. Before serving, heat in microwave, stir to fluff, add lemon juice, hot cream, and fresh herbs.

OK, it is not a misprint! Yes, there *is* a pinch (or a "kiss," as I'd prefer to call it) of sugar sprinkled on the hot, cooked asparagus. It just adds a special "something" that enhances the flavor. Try it on other vegetables—squash, green beans, sugar snap peas, carrots, and cabbage. You'll swear by it!

Oven-Roasted Asparagus

Serves 6

1½ lbs	**Fresh asparagus, rinsed in cold water**
3 Tbsp	**Olive oil**
½ tsp	**Salt** *(sea salt if possible)*
Pinch	**Sugar**
	Zest *(grated peel)* **of one large lemon**

Preheat broiler. With one hand at the root end of an asparagus stalk and the other hand ¾ of the way up the stalk, bend gently. The asparagus will snap where the tough portion ends. *If the asparagus is especially large you may want to peel the stem with a vegetable peeler to make it more tender.* Discard the tough end, and either continue snapping each spear, **or** make an executive decision and cut them all off evenly with a knife. This isn't rocket science—keep things in perspective. It's just asparagus!!

Spread out asparagus spears in a single layer on a jelly-roll pan. Drizzle with oil and roll to coat all sides. Place under the broiler, about 3 inches below the element, and broil for 4 minutes only. Remove from oven. Sprinkle with salt and kiss of sugar and place on a serving platter or individual plates. Sprinkle with lemon zest and serve immediately.

Variation: Instead of broiling in the oven, grill the asparagus over direct heat on your outdoor grill. Place the oiled spears on a clean grill. Cook about 3 minutes *(you should have pretty grill marks)*, turn, and cook until tender-crisp. Remove from grill and continue as directed.

Make-Ahead Tip: The day before, trim asparagus, place on a baking sheet, and oil the spears. Cover and refrigerate. Zest lemon, cover, and refrigerate. Before broiling, remove the baking pan from the refrigerator and allow to come to room temperature, about 30 minutes. Proceed as directed.

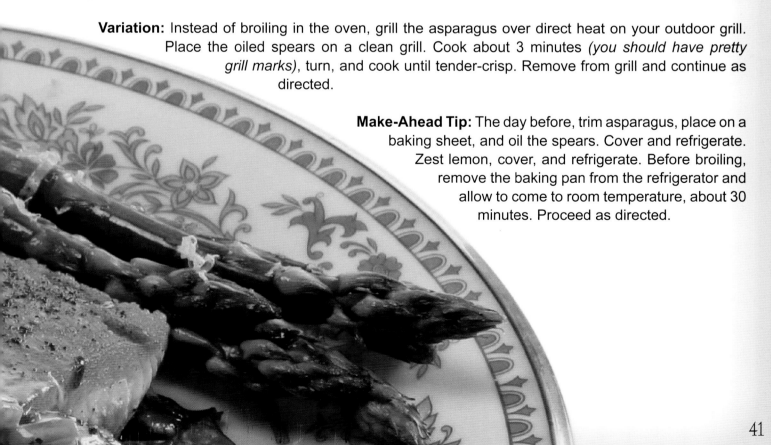

Tropical Tart

Serves 10-12

Crust:

1 (9")	**Pie crust** *(I prefer the rolled type in the refrigerated section)*

Filling:

8 oz	**Cream cheese, softened**
⅓ Cup	**Sugar**
1 tsp	**Pure vanilla extract**
1 Large	**Lemon, zested**
1 Tbsp	**Lemon juice**

Topping:

¼ -½ Cup	**Pineapple preserves**
1 Tbsp	**Grated fresh gingerroot**
2 Large	**Ripe** *(but firm)* **bananas, peeled**
¼ Cup	**Chopped macadamia nuts**
¼ Cup	**Sweetened flaked coconut**
	Lemon slices and fresh mint leaves to garnish

Fyi...

Removable-Bottom Tart Pans

Keep a variety of sizes on hand. They make anything baked in them look special because of the scalloped sides. The top edges are quite sharp, so be careful when lining the pans. Any crust that extends over the sides can be cut off evenly by rolling a rolling pin across the top of the pan. Voila! A perfect crust! Place the pan on a baking sheet before cooking. This makes it much easier to get it in and out of the oven without damaging the crust.

To prepare the crust: Preheat oven to 375°. Line a 9-inch removable-bottom tart pan with the crust, then line crust with parchment. Fill with pie weights or dried beans, and bake 15 minutes. Remove parchment and weights. Return to oven and bake 5-8 minutes more or until golden. Cool.

To prepare the filling: Beat together the cream cheese, sugar, vanilla, lemon zest, and lemon juice until smooth. Spread mixture evenly over the bottom of the cooked and cooled crust.

To prepare the topping: Preheat the broiler. In a small saucepan or in the microwave, melt the preserves with the grated gingerroot. Thinly slice the bananas, and arrange decoratively over the cream cheese filling. Brush with the preserve mixture and sprinkle with the macadamia nuts and coconut. Broil until nuts and coconut are golden, about 2-3 minutes. Watch carefully, as the coconut can burn! Refrigerate tart and chill completely, about 2 hours. Slice with a sharp knife, wiping the blade before each cut. Garnish with lemon slices and fresh mint. Store remaining tart in the refrigerator.

Make-Ahead Tip: This tart is best when served the day it is made. Prepare early in the day and refrigerate until serving time. Refrigerate sliced lemon and washed mint sprigs for garnish.

"Be prepared!"—The perfect motto for the hostess.

4 Days Before:	Follow up on RSVPs; verify number of guests.
3 Days Before:	Gather and make ready all table linens, dishes, flatware, glasses, serving utensils, salt and pepper grinders, plan or order centerpiece, decide on all beverages.
2 Days Before:	Edit grocery list; shop for all items EXCEPT fresh salmon, purchase wines, spirits, and liqueurs.
	Set the table—completely!
	Prepare pecans for salad.
1 Day Before:	Purchase fresh salmon, season, and brown in skillet. Refrigerate on a baking sheet. Make Wine-Shallot Sauce; refrigerate. Wash spinach, slice shallots.
	Make vinaigrette; refrigerate in a squeeze bottle. Wash salad greens.
	Cook rice with zest, broth, and salt. Juice lemon and mince herbs.
	Trim asparagus, place in sheet pan with oil; zest lemon; refrigerate.
Party Day:	**This will be fun!**
Early Afternoon:	Slice pears and cover with lemon-lime soda; refrigerate.
	Prepare tropical tart; refrigerate. Prepare lemon slices and mint for garnish.
30-45 Minutes Before:	Remove salmon, sauce, spinach, and shallots from the refrigerator, preheat oven. Heat the sauce in the microwave or on top of the stove.
	Remove rice from refrigerator, heat in microwave; heat cream. When the rice is hot, stir in lemon juice, herbs, and cream.

Remove asparagus from refrigerator; preheat broiler.

Plate salad and serve.

After Clearing Salad: After clearing salad, bake salmon for 10 minutes; broil asparagus and finish with zest, sugar, and sea salt; wilt spinach, rewarm rice if necessary.

Prepare plates.

Serve tropical tart.

Elegant Dinner for Friends

For 6 people

Produce

☐	2	Ripe *(but firm)* pears
☐	2	Ripe *(but firm)* bananas
☐	3 Large	Lemons
☐	1½ lbs	Fresh asparagus
☐	1 Stalk	Celery
☐	6-8 Cups	Mixed greens for salad
☐	1½ - 2 lbs	Fresh baby spinach
☐	8 oz	Sliced button mushrooms
☐	1 Clove	Garlic
☐	4 Large	Shallots
☐	2 Tbsp	Fresh minced tarragon or Italian flat-leaf parsley for salad garnish
☐	4 Tbsp	Fresh minced tarragon or 4 tsp dried tarragon
☐	2 Tbsp	Fresh minced herbs *(parsley, dill, tarragon, basil, or a combination)*
☐		Mint leaves to garnish Tropical Tart
☐	1 Tbsp	Grated fresh gingerroot

Dairy & Eggs

☐	9 Tbsp	Unsalted butter
☐	1¼ Cups	Whipping cream

Cheese & Deli

☐	8 oz	Roquefort cheese, crumbled
☐	8 oz	Cream cheese

Meat & Fish

☐	6 (4-oz)	Salmon fillets, skinless

Canned Vegetables, Fruits, & Dried Fruits

☐	2 Cups	Chicken broth

Pasta, Grains, & Cereals

☐	1 Cup	Long grain rice

Baking, Spices, & Nuts

☐	1 Cup	Sugar

☐	1 tsp	Pure vanilla extract
☐	1 tsp	Dry mustard
☐		Cayenne *(optional)*
☐		Salt and pepper to taste
☐	½ tsp	Salt *(sea salt if possible)* for asparagus
☐	1½ Cups	Pecans, halves or chopped
☐	¼ Cup	Chopped macadamia nuts, chopped
☐	¼ Cup	Sweetened flaked coconut

Condiments

☐	7 Tbsp	Olive oil
☐	1 Cup	Canola oil *(or light olive oil or grape seed oil)*
☐	⅓ Cup	Apple cider vinegar
☐	Dash	Hot sauce
☐	¼ - ½ Cup	Pineapple preserves

Breads

☐	1 (9")	Pie crust *(I prefer the rolled type in refrigerated section)*

Miscellaneous

☐	1 liter	Lemon-lime soda *(to soak pears after slicing)*

Wine & Spirits

☐	1 Cup	Champagne or dry white wine
☐		Full-Bodied Chardonnay *(recommended wine for meal)*

Easy Italian

Molly's Sensational
Caesar Salad

Manicotti

Garlic-Sautéed Spinach

Tony's Toast

Tiramisu

Italian Barbera
or a
Light Chianti

Everyone loves Italian food—and somehow, an occasion always becomes more festive when the flavors of Italy are on the menu! The mood is set when the guests walk in the door—who can resist that wonderful aroma of garlic, basil, and tomato?

I find it helps to have a theme for a dinner party. That makes it so easy to decorate and create the perfect ambience. Create a casual pizza-parlor feel with a red-and-white-checked tablecloth or napkins, or perhaps several straw-covered Chianti bottles as candleholders. For a more sophisticated mood, use Italian ceramic plates and table linens to complement the colors of the plates. Before you know it, you've brought a neighborhood trattoria into your own dining room! Play some Italian music and you're set for a good time.

I've always loved using components of a meal in different ways. The dressing for the salad makes a great sandwich spread. Add grilled chicken, a leaf of romaine, and a sprinkle of Parmesan, and you have a yummy Chicken Caesar Sandwich! The sauce for the manicotti is a good, all-purpose pasta sauce—great over spaghetti. Instead of making manicotti, you could use lasagna noodles and layer the sauce and the ricotta filling. Remember the rule...make it easy and stress free! Since the pasta dish can be frozen—as long as you're cooking, you may as well double it! Set one aside for the freezer and you have a delicious future dinner at your fingertips!

Pour a glass of Chianti and enjoy! *Mangia! Mangia!*

This Caesar Salad is our family favorite. Kevin, Kelly, and I worked long and hard taste-testing to create what we think is the very best in the universe! Don't omit the anchovies...they are essential to the overall flavor! I hope you love it too!

Molly's Sensational Caesar Salad

Dressing:

Makes 1⅓ Cups

6	**Anchovy fillets** *(canned)*
2	**Egg yolks**
2 Cloves	**Garlic, minced**
½ Cup	**Grated Parmesan cheese**
3 Tbsp	**Red wine vinegar**
3 Tbsp	**Lime juice**
2 tsp	**Dijon mustard**
1 tsp	**Worcestershire sauce**
6 Dashes	**Hot sauce**
1 tsp	**Salt**
1 tsp	**Freshly ground black pepper**
½ Cup	**Olive oil**
½ Cup	**Canola oil**

Salad:

Romaine lettuce, torn into bite-size pieces
Croutons *(best if homemade!)*
Additional Parmesan cheese to garnish

To prepare the dressing: Combine everything except oils in a food processor and blend until smooth. With machine running, slowly pour in oils in a slow, steady stream. Mixture will emulsify and thicken. Taste and add salt and pepper as needed.

To prepare the salad: Place crisp, clean romaine and croutons in a salad bowl. Add dressing sparingly (you want to lightly coat the salad), toss together, and top with additional Parmesan cheese. Pass remaining dressing.

Make-Ahead Tip: A day ahead, prepare the salad dressing and store in the refrigerator. Have romaine clean and torn, and refrigerated in a zip-top bag. Croutons can be made a couple of days in advance *(careful, though...you will find it very tempting to walk by and sample a few).*

How To ...

Make Homemade Croutons:

1 Loaf	Italian bread *(or any other sturdy bread)*, cut into 1-inch cubes
2 Tbsp	Olive oil
2 Tbsp	Unsalted butter, melted
2 Cloves	Garlic, pressed
2-3 tsp	Dried Italian seasoning
	Kosher salt

Preheat oven to 375°. In a large mixing bowl, stir together the olive oil, butter, and garlic. Add bread cubes and quickly toss to coat. Pour out in a single layer onto a greased baking sheet. Sprinkle with dried Italian seasoning and kosher salt. Bake in oven for 10 - 12 minutes until crisp and golden brown, stirring occasionally. Remove from oven and let cool completely. Store in an airtight container.

Manicotti

Serves 6-8

al dente

Italians are serious about their pasta. It should be cooked al dente, meaning "to the tooth". Cooked pasta should have a bit of resistance as you chew it; done, but not over-cooked and mushy. Cooking times vary depending on the use of fresh or dried pasta, and the type and size of pasta. I usually rely on the cooking instructions printed on the package. Boil pasta in plenty of salted water for the minimum amount of time then check by tasting. Drain the pasta after cooking *(but never rinse it, as this would carry away the starch that helps sauce to "cling").* You can also reserve up to half a cup of the drained liquid to recombine with the pasta. The starch in the liquid will also help the pasta to "grip" the sauce.

Sauce:

2 Tbsp	Olive oil
½ lb	Ground beef
½ lb	Bulk Italian sausage, mild or spicy
1 Large	Onion, diced
2 Cloves	Garlic, pressed
8 oz	Sliced button mushrooms
32 oz	Tomato sauce
1 (1.5-oz) Pkg	Spaghetti sauce mix
1 tsp	Dried basil *(or 1 tablespoon minced fresh)*
1 tsp	Dried oregano *(or 1 tablespoon minced fresh)*
1½ tsp	Anise seed, crushed

Manicotti Shells:

2 Tbsp	Minced Italian flat-leaf parsley *(or fresh basil)*
1 (10-oz) Pkg	Frozen chopped spinach, thawed and squeezed dry
1 lb	Ricotta cheese
2 Large	Eggs, beaten
½ tsp	Salt
	Ground pepper to taste
1 Cup	Grated mozzarella cheese
½ Cup	Grated Parmesan cheese
8 oz	Manicotti shells, cooked al dente

Topping for Assembly:

1 Cup	Grated mozzarella cheese
½ Cup	Grated Parmesan cheese
	Additional parsley or basil to garnish

To prepare the sauce: Heat olive oil in a large Dutch oven or stockpot. Brown ground meat and sausage until cooked through. Drain if necessary. Add onions, garlic, and mushrooms and cook until onion is tender, about 5 minutes. Stir in the tomato sauce, spaghetti sauce mix, dried or fresh herbs, and anise seeds. Simmer covered for about 30 minutes, stirring occasionally.

To prepare the manicotti shells: In a medium mixing bowl, combine the parsley, spinach, ricotta, eggs, salt, pepper, and the cheeses. Fill cooked manicotti shells generously with the mixture. The easiest way is if you use a pastry bag fitted with a large open tip, or a long iced tea spoon. Fill to the middle from one end, then turn shell around and fill from the other end!

To assemble: In a 9 x 13-inch greased casserole dish, spread enough of the meat sauce to coat the bottom. Arrange the filled shells in a single layer on top of the sauce, cover with the remaining sauce, and sprinkle with the remaining cheeses. Bake at 350° for about 30 minutes or until bubbly. Serve hot, garnished with minced parsley or basil.

Make-Ahead Tip: Assemble manicotti the day before, but do not top with cheese. Refrigerate. To serve, bake covered for 30 minutes, uncover and sprinkle with cheeses, and bake uncovered for 30 more minutes.

Garlic Sautéed Spinach

Serves 6-8

3 Tbsp	Olive oil
2	Shallots, minced
1 Clove	Garlic, minced
2½ lbs	Fresh baby spinach, washed
1 (6-oz) Jar	Marinated artichoke hearts, drained and chopped
¼ Cup	Pine nuts, toasted *(see How to... on page 28)*

Heat olive oil in a large sauté pan or wok until hot. Add shallots, garlic, and spinach, and quickly stir until spinach wilts. Add artichoke hearts and cook until warmed through. Use a slotted spoon to serve, as cooked spinach produces a lot of water. Top with pine nuts before serving.

Make-Ahead Tip: The day before, have shallots and garlic chopped. Store them together in a zip-top bag in the refrigerator. Drain and chop the artichoke hearts. Wash the spinach; toast the pine nuts.

Fyi...

Fresh Spinach...

Fresh spinach has a high moisture content, and greatly decreases in volume when it is cooked. To help you gauge quantities for serving, keep in mind that a pound of fresh spinach is about 10-11 cups. When cooked, it becomes about 1½ cups or about 3 servings.

Who's Tony? Who knows? (Who cares?) Rumor has it he was some Italian guy from Denver. This bread is crisp, golden, and so tasty. Believe me, this is not your run-of-the-mill garlic bread. While this is baking, the aroma is absolutely intoxicating!

Tony's Toast

About 10 slices

1 Small	**Loaf Italian bread, sliced on the diagonal into 1-inch-thick slices**
1 Cup	**Milk** *(2% or whole)*
½ Cup	**Unsalted butter, melted**
2 Cloves	**Garlic, pressed**
2-3 Cups	**Grated** *(not shredded)* **Parmesan cheese**

Preheat oven to 425°. Warm the milk with butter and garlic and place in a shallow bowl. You will need to stir often to keep the mixture from separating. Pour cheese into shallow bowl. Quickly dip each side of bread first into milk then into cheese to completely coat. The idea is to **moisten** each side of the bread with the milk-butter-garlic mixture, not soak it as you would French toast! Place bread slices on a generously oiled baking sheet. *Brush with oil—do not spray with no-stick cooking spray!* Bake for 5-7 minutes. Turn toast over and bake until golden. Serve hot.

Make-Ahead Tip: Early on the day of your dinner, dip and coat bread slices and place on the prepared baking sheet. Cover and refrigerate. Before baking, remove from the refrigerator and allow to warm to room temperature, about 30 minutes.

Tiramisu

Serves 8-10

Ladyfingers:

3 (3-oz) Pkg	Ladyfingers
⅓ Cup	Brewed espresso coffee, cooled
2 Tbsp	Brandy, dark rum, or sweet marsala

Cream layer:

6 Large	Eggs, separated *(be sure to use fresh eggs)*
6 Tbsp	Sugar
1 tsp	Pure vanilla extract
2 lbs	Mascarpone cheese OR 1½ lbs cream cheese mixed with ½ Cup heavy cream and ¼ Cup sour cream
4 Tbsp	Unsweetened cocoa powder
	Chocolate-covered espresso beans to garnish

To prepare the ladyfingers: Separate the ladyfingers and spread out in a single layer on a large baking sheet. In a small bowl, combine coffee and brandy. Sprinkle ladyfingers with mixture and set aside.

To prepare the cream layer: In a medium bowl, beat egg yolks and sugar with an electric mixer on medium-high speed until thick and lemon-colored *(about 4-5 minutes)*. **Set your timer—this step is important!** Add mascarpone cheese and blend on low speed until combined.

In a large bowl, beat egg whites with electric mixer and the wire whip attachment on medium-high speed until soft peaks form (2-3 minutes). Stir about a third of the beaten egg whites into the mascarpone mixture to lighten. Using a large rubber spatula, fold the remaining egg whites into mascarpone mixture.

To assemble: Line the bottom of a buttered 9 x 13-inch deep casserole dish with half the ladyfingers, covering completely. Spread half the mascarpone mixture over the ladyfingers and sift 2 Tbsp of cocoa over the surface. Repeat with remaining half of ladyfingers and mascarpone mixture, ending with cocoa. Cover with plastic wrap and refrigerate for at least 2 hours or overnight. To serve, cut or spoon out onto dessert plates dusted with a bit of cocoa. Chocolate-covered espresso beans make a pretty garnish.

Variation: This is not a real sweet dessert. If desired, you can increase the amount of sugar to 8-10 Tbsp.

Make-Ahead Tip: Prepare the Tiramisu the day before you plan to serve it. Store tightly covered in the refrigerator.

Your guests have the best time when you get to be part of the fun, too!

4 Days Before:	Follow up on RSVPs; verify number of guests.

3 Days Before: Gather and make ready all table linens, dishes, flatware, glasses, serving utensils, salt and pepper grinders; plan or order centerpiece; decide on all beverages.

2 Days Before: Edit grocery list; shop for all items, including wines, spirits, and liqueurs.

Set the table—completely!

Make croutons for salad; store in zip-top bag.

1 Day Before: Prepare salad dressing; wash and tear romaine lettuce, store in refrigerator.

Prepare and assemble manicotti, but do not top with cheeses. Cover and refrigerate.

Wash spinach; chop the shallots, garlic, and artichokes; toast the pine nuts; refrigerate.

Prepare the Tiramisu; cover tightly and refrigerate.

Party Day! Buon appetito!

Early Afternoon: Slice and dip bread for Tony's Toast; refrigerate on oiled sheet pan.

1½ Hours Before: Remove manicotti from refrigerator; preheat oven to 350°; bake manicotti as directed.

Remove ingredients for the spinach dish from refrigerator.

Remove bread for toast from refrigerator; when the manicotti is finished, increase the oven temperature to 425°.

30 Minutes Before: Bake Tony's Toast; toss salad.

Sauté spinach.

Brew coffee.

Serve dinner! Have a glass of wine for your job well done!

Serve Tiramisu.

Easy Italian

For 6-8 people

Produce

- [ ] 3 Large   Limes
- [ ] 2½ lbs   Fresh baby spinach
- [ ] 6-8 Cups   Romaine lettuce
- [ ] 8 oz   Sliced button mushrooms
- [ ] 9 Cloves   Garlic
- [ ] 1 Large   Onion
- [ ] 2   Shallots
- [ ] 2 Tbsp   Fresh minced Italian flat-leaf parsley or fresh minced basil
- [ ] 1 Tbsp   Fresh Italian flat-leaf parsley & fresh basil to garnish manicotti

Dairy & Eggs

- [ ] 10 Tbsp   Unsalted butter
- [ ] 1 Cup   Milk *(2% or whole)*
- [ ] 10 Large   Eggs

Cheese & Deli

- [ ] 4½ Cups   Grated Parmesan cheese
- [ ] ½ Cup   Shredded Parmesan cheese
- [ ] 1 lb   Ricotta cheese
- [ ] 2 Cups   Grated mozzarella cheese
- [ ] 2 lbs   Mascarpone cheese
  OR 1½ lbs cream cheese mixed with ½ Cup heavy cream and ¼ Cup sour cream

Meat & Fish

- [ ] ½ lb   Ground beef
- [ ] ½ lb   Bulk Italian sausage, mild or spicy

Canned Vegetables, Fruits, & Dried Fruits

- [ ] 6   Anchovy filets *(canned; usually about 12 filets per can)*
- [ ] 32 oz   Tomato sauce
- [ ] 1 (6-oz) Jar   Marinated artichoke hearts

Pasta, Grains, Cereal
- [ ] 8 oz — Manicotti shells

Baking, Spices, & Nuts
- [ ] 6 Tbsp — Sugar *(additional 8-10 Tbsp for Tiramisu optional)*
- [ ] 1 tsp — Pure vanilla extract
- [ ] 4 Tbsp — Unsweetened cocoa powder
- [ ] 1 (1.5-oz) Pkg — Spaghetti sauce mix
- [ ] 2-3 tsp — Dried Italian seasoning
- [ ] 1 tsp — Dried basil or 1 Tbsp fresh basil for manicotti sauce
- [ ] 1 tsp — Dried oregano or 1 Tbsp fresh oregano for manicotti sauce
- [ ] 1½ tsp — Anise seed, crushed
- [ ] ¼ Cup — Pine nuts

Condiments
- [ ] 1 Cup — Olive oil
- [ ] ½ Cup — Canola oil
- [ ] 3 Tbsp — Red wine vinegar
- [ ] 2 tsp — Dijon mustard
- [ ] 1 tsp — Worcestershire sauce
- [ ] 6 Dashes — Hot sauce

Breads
- [ ] 2 — Loaves Italian bread *(or any sturdy bread)*
- [ ] 3 (3-oz) Pkg — Ladyfingers

Freezer
- [ ] 1 (10-oz) Pkg — Frozen chopped spinach

Miscellaneous
- [ ] ⅓ Cup — Brewed espresso coffee
- [ ] — Chocolate-covered espresso beans for Tiramisu garnish

Wine & Spirits
- [ ] 2 Tbsp — Brandy, dark rum, or sweet marsala
- [ ] — Italian Barbera or a Light Chianti *(recommended wine for meal)*

Sunday
Family Dinner

Salad with Greek Goddess Dressing

Perfect Roast Chicken with Gravy

Oven-Glazed Carrots

Molly's Mashed Potatoes
Or...
Rosemary-Roasted New Potatoes

Steamed Green Vegetable
of your choice

Apple Pie in a Sack

Pinot Noir

The thought of Sunday dinner puts a smile on my face. My happiest memories always seem to involve family and friends gathered around the table. Sharing good food, conversation, and laughter with those we hold most dear is the ultimate joy. Make time to be with your loved ones. We all have busy schedules, but don't be too busy for your friends or your family. They are your greatest treasures.

From the moment they walk in the door, they will feel at home. The aroma of a perfectly roasted chicken is simply hard to beat. This is pure comfort food—very down-home and delicious. It's always a good idea to test the temperature of the chicken to make certain it has reached 160°-165°. A good thermometer will prevent disaster. I vividly remember overcooking a prime rib roast one Christmas! If you want this to be the ultimate Southern Sunday dinner, serve with mashed potatoes. If you're feeling more sophisticated, try the Rosemary-Roasted New Potatoes instead. (I've given you a choice.) When choosing your green vegetable, keep in mind our rule about the textures of the individual foods on the plate. Variety is the key to a happy and contented eye and palate!

For dessert—positively the *best* apple pie. And yes, it's baked in a sack! This is a recipe from Dorothy, a dear family friend from Midland, Texas. It is delicious served warm with a scoop of vanilla ice cream.

Dear Lord, bless this food, this family, and these friends. Please pass the chicken. Amen!

This was my mom's salad bowl, made during WWII. Note the inscription on the base: "MADE IN AMERICA FOR AMERICANS"!

This salad stimulates the palate. The lemon is bright and lively; the bacon tastes like home. A definite "Diva" or, in this case, "Goddess" type of salad!

Salad with Greek Goddess Dressing

(*Not to be confused with Green Goddess!!*)

Serves 6-8

Fyi...
Juice and Zest Yields from Lemons and Limes

One medium lemon will yield 2-3 Tbsp juice and 2-3 tsp zest; one medium lime will yield 1-2 Tbsp juice and 1-2 tsp zest.

Salad:

2 Heads	Romaine lettuce, washed and torn into bite-size pieces
1 (6-oz) Jar	Marinated artichoke hearts, drained and chopped
6 Slices	Bacon, diced, cooked crisp, and drained
3	Roma tomatoes, sliced
1 Cup	Homemade croutons (see How to...page 51)
½ Cup	Shredded Romano cheese (or Parmesan, if you prefer)

Dressing:

1 Clove	Garlic, minced
6 Tbsp	Freshly squeezed lemon juice
2	Egg yolks
1 Tbsp	Finely minced fresh mint
2 tsp	Finely minced fresh oregano
Dash	Hot sauce
1 Cup	Extra-virgin olive oil
	Salt and pepper to taste

To prepare the salad: In a large bowl, combine the lettuce, artichoke hearts, bacon, and tomatoes. Toss with enough dressing to lightly coat the lettuce leaves. Divide among chilled salad plates; top with croutons and shredded Romano cheese.

To prepare the dressing: In the bowl of a food processor or blender, combine the garlic, lemon juice, egg yolks, mint, oregano, and hot sauce until smooth. With the machine running, add olive oil in a slow, steady stream until dressing is emulsified. Adjust seasonings.

Make-Ahead Tip: Make croutons two days in advance and store in an airtight container. Prepare lettuce and vegetables for the salad a day in advance. Store all ingredients separately in zip-top bags in the refrigerator. Prepare dressing one day in advance; store in the refrigerator.

Fyi...
Use of Raw Egg Yolks

I must admit...I am not too worried about making a salad dressing with raw egg yolks. I always use fresh, refrigerated eggs purchased a couple of days before use. Over the last several years, many measures have been taken to reduce the prevalence of salmonella. There is no guarantee that all eggs are bacteria free, however. I realize that many people are concerned, especially when dealing with pregnant women, the elderly, or individuals with weakened immune systems, so here is my suggestion: either use a pasteurized egg or egg product in place of the raw yolk, or eliminate the yolk and prepare the salad dressing as a vinaigrette. The texture will be different but the flavor is still great. If you opt to use the raw yolks, tell your guests so they can decide whether to consume the dressing—and have an alternate dressing on hand for them. There is no need to stress; this takes all the fun out of entertaining, so do what makes you comfortable.

How To ...

Hints and Tips for Working with Chicken

When at all possible, choose a roasting hen, not a fryer. Roasting hens are larger and fatter, which keeps the meat moist and juicy throughout the roasting process and gives you better drippings for your gravy.

Place your cutting board in a rimmed baking sheet. When you carve the chicken, the baking sheet will catch the juices and prevent them from running all over your countertop!

Be sure to sanitize everything that comes in contact with raw poultry juices, such as knives, cutting boards, and countertops. Use a very mild bleach solution to ensure the elimination of all bacteria.

Perfect Roast Chicken with Gravy and Oven-Glazed Carrots

Serves 8-10

Chickens:

2 Large	Red onions, peeled, and thickly and evenly sliced
3 Stalks	Celery, sliced in 2-inch pieces
2	Roasting hens, 5-6 pounds each
	Salt and lemon pepper
8 Sprigs	Fresh thyme or rosemary
2 Large	Lemons, each cut in half
2 Bulbs	Garlic, each cut in half
1 Medium	Onion, quartered
6 Tbsp	Unsalted butter, melted

Carrots:

2 lbs	Baby carrots

Gravy:

2 Cups	Chicken broth
4 Tbsp	All-purpose flour
	Salt and pepper to taste

To prepare the chickens and carrots: Preheat oven to 425°. Place onion slices and celery in a single layer in the bottom of a large open roasting pan, one that is NOT nonstick! These will act as a rack for the chickens, keeping them off the bottom of the pan. We want to encourage browning. Clean hens, removing giblets and any excess fat. Tuck wings under. Pat the outside dry with paper towels. Place the hens in the roasting pan, on top of the onions and celery! Salt and pepper the cavities of each hen generously. Place half the herbs, lemons, garlic, and onion in each hen. Brush the outside of the birds with the melted butter. Sprinkle the outside with a bit more salt and lemon pepper. Tie the legs together with cotton kitchen twine. Roast the hens uncovered for about 1 hour. Add carrots to the bottom of the roaster, stirring to coat with pan drippings. Return to the oven and roast 30-45 minutes more or until the carrots are browned and tender, and the chickens are cooked through. The internal temperature should reach about 165° and juices should run clear. Remove chickens *(and any vegetables)* to a platter, tent with foil, and keep warm.

To prepare the gravy: Remove all but about 4 Tbsp of fat from the bottom of the roasting pan. Heat roasting pan over medium high heat, and stir in flour. Using a whisk, cook and stir for about 2-3 minutes. Add chicken broth, and stir the bottom of the pan to release all the browned bits. Let simmer to thicken. Taste and add salt and pepper as needed. Serve over sliced chicken.

Make-Ahead Tip: In the early afternoon of your party day, prepare the hens for roasting and have them ready in the pan. Refrigerate until about 30 minutes before you put them in the oven.

These are good, buttery, creamy potatoes—the perfect Southern accompaniment to our roast chicken. Not a fan of garlic? Leave it out. Either way, these are delicious!

Molly's Mashed Potatoes

Serves 8

Roasted Garlic:

2 Bulbs	Garlic
2 Tsp	Olive oil
⅓ Cup	Chicken broth

Potatoes:

5 Large	Russet potatoes *(about 2-2½ lbs)*
2 tsp	Kosher salt
8 Tbsp	Unsalted butter, melted
½ to ¾ Cup	Milk *(2% or whole)*, heated
2 Tbsp	Minced fresh chives *(optional)*
	Salt and pepper to taste

To prepare the roasted garlic: Preheat oven to 375°. Cut off tops of garlic bulbs to expose cloves. Drizzle with olive oil. Place in small oven-proof dish. Pour chicken broth over the garlic and cover tightly with foil. Bake for 30 minutes or until very tender. Squeeze out each garlic clove, mash, and set aside. Reserve broth in pan.

To prepare the potatoes: Peel and dice potatoes. In a large saucepan or stockpot, cover potatoes with cold water and bring to a boil. Add salt. Reduce heat to simmer, then cover, cooking until tender when pierced with a fork, about 20 minutes. Drain. In the bowl of an electric mixer, combine potatoes, roasted garlic, reserved chicken broth, and melted butter. Whip until fluffy. Add milk as needed to reach desired consistency. Stir in fresh minced chives if desired. Taste and adjust seasonings.

Make-Ahead Tip: Prepare potatoes a couple of hours in advance and keep warm, covered, in a heat-resistant bowl over simmering water. They won't taste like reheated potatoes!
Or... try these instead

Rosemary-Roasted New Potatoes
Serves 6-8

1½ lbs	Small new potatoes, scrubbed and halved or quartered
2 Tbsp	Melted butter
2 Tbsp	Olive oil
1 Tbsp	Minced fresh rosemary
	Salt and pepper

Preheat oven to 375°. Place potatoes in a shallow roasting pan. Add butter, olive oil, and rosemary. Stir to coat. Season with salt and pepper and bake until potatoes are tender and golden, about 30 minutes. Stir occasionally.

Make-Ahead Tip: Coat the potatoes with the butter, oil, and rosemary. Place on baking sheet a couple of hours before roasting. Cover and leave at room temperature until time to place in the oven.

While this pie is baking, the aromas wafting from the kitchen will make you crazy with anticipation. It is such a familiar, homey fragrance. If you think it smells good, just wait 'til you taste it!

Apple Pie in a Sack

Serves 8

Pie Crust:

1½ Cups	*All-purpose flour*
½ tsp	*Salt*
½ Cup	*Vegetable shortening* (I use Crisco)
4-5 Tbsp	*Ice water*

Filling:

6 Large	*Apples, peeled, cored, and thinly sliced* (I use Granny Smiths)
1 tsp	*Pure vanilla extract*
¾ Cup	*Sugar*
3 Tbsp	*All-purpose flour*
½ tsp	*Grated fresh whole nutmeg or ground nutmeg*
1 tsp	*Ground cinnamon*

Topping:

½ Cup	*Sugar*
½ tsp	*Ground cinnamon*
½ Cup	*All-purpose flour*
½ Cup	*Chopped pecans, toasted*
6 Tbsp	*Unsalted butter, very cold, cut into small cubes*

To prepare the crust: In the bowl of a food processor, pulse the flour and salt to evenly distribute ingredients. Add shortening, and pulse until the mixture resembles oatmeal. Sprinkle with the 4 Tbsp of ice water, then pulse to combine. Add more ice water if needed. Shape into a disc and chill for 20 minutes. Roll out on a lightly floured surface to 1/8-inch thick. Transfer to a 9-inch deep pie dish. Turn edges under and flute. Refrigerate until filling is ready.

To prepare filling: In a large bowl, combine the prepared apples and vanilla. In a separate bowl, stir together the remaining filling ingredients to evenly distribute all ingredients. Pour over apples and stir to combine thoroughly. Pour filling into uncooked pie crust, mounding apples in the center.

The Dining Diva

To prepare topping: Place the sugar, cinnamon, flour, and pecans in the bowl of a food processor; pulse to combine. Quickly pulse in the chilled butter until the mixture is crumbly. Evenly distribute on top of the apple filling in the crust.

To bake: Preheat oven to 425°. Place a brown paper grocery bag on a baking sheet, put the pie in it, and close with metal paper clips. Place in lower third of the oven, taking care that the sack doesn't touch the top oven element. Bake for 55 minutes. Carefully remove the pie from the bag and allow it to cool to desired temperature. Serve with cinnamon or vanilla ice cream. You'll have a perfect ending to your Sunday dinner.

Make-Ahead Tip: Bake the pie early in the afternoon of your dinner party. Warm about 10 minutes in a 350° oven before serving if desired. Store leftover pie in the refrigerator.

One Week Before:	Order roasting hens if they are not normally available where you shop.
4 Days Before:	Follow up on RSVPs; verify number of guests.
3 Days Before:	Gather and make ready all table linens, dishes, flatware, glasses, serving utensils, and salt and pepper grinders; plan or order centerpiece; decide on all beverages.
2 Days Before:	Edit grocery list; shop for all items; purchase wines, spirits, and liqueurs.
	Set the table—completely!
	Make croutons for salad; store in zip-top bag.
1 Day Before:	Make salad dressing and refrigerate. Wash and prepare lettuce; prepare all vegetables for salad; fry bacon, store separately in zip-top bags in the refrigerator
	Roast garlic for potatoes, extract cloves, mash, and store in refrigerator tightly covered, with the broth they were cooked in. Peel and dice potatoes, store covered with water and 2 Tbsp lemon juice to prevent browning; refrigerate.
	Prepare green vegetable of choice to have ready for steaming.
	Make pie crust dough, wrap in plastic, and refrigerate. Peel and slice apples; store in refrigerator submerged in lemon-lime soda. Prepare topping for pie and refrigerate in a zip-top bag.
Party Day:	**Family Time!**
Early Afternoon:	Assemble and bake pie. After it has cooled completely, store at room temperature, lightly covered.
	Prepare hens and place in roasting pan.
3 Hours Before:	Preheat oven to 425°. Roast hens. When done, place on ovenproof platter and keep warm in oven set at 150°-200°.
	Make gravy and transfer to microwaveable container or a saucepan.
	After hens go in to roast, drain potatoes from acidulated water,

cover with fresh cold water, cook and prepare Mashed Potatoes. Transfer to a heat-resistant glass (or stainless steel) bowl, cover, and keep warm over a saucepan of barely simmering water.

30 Minutes Before:
Slice chickens and return to warm oven.

Assemble salad; put green vegetable in to steam; serve salad.

After clearing salad, remove chicken platter from oven. Heat gravy in microwave. Transfer potatoes and green vegetable to serving dishes. Serve.

Clear table; brew coffee. Warm pie and serve with ice cream.

Leisurely enjoy your loved ones! You might want to take a picture or two, or even a video. You will enjoy seeing the faces and hearing the voices in years to come.

Sunday Family Dinner

For 8 People

Produce

☐	6	Lemons *(including lemon for acidulating water for potatoes)*
☐	6 Large	Apples *(I prefer Granny Smith)*
☐	3	Roma tomatoes
☐	2-3 Heads	Romaine lettuce
☐	5 Bulbs	Garlic
☐	2 Large	Red onions
☐	1 Medium	Onion
☐	5 Large	Russet potatoes *(about 2-2 ½ lbs)*
☐	1½ lbs	Small new potatoes *(if you are making the Roasted New Potatoes)*
☐	3 Stalks	Celery
☐	2 lbs	Baby carrots
☐		Green vegetable of your choice
☐	1 Tbsp	Fresh minced mint
☐	2 tsp	Fresh minced oregano
☐	8 Sprigs	Fresh thyme or rosemary *(additional 1 Tbsp if you are making the Roasted New Potatoes)*
☐	2 Tbsp	Fresh minced chives *(optional for mashed potatoes)*

Dairy & Eggs

☐	1½ Cups	Unsalted Butter
☐	½ - ¾ Cup	Milk *(2% or whole)*
☐	2 Large	Eggs

Cheese & Deli

☐	½ Cup	Shredded Romano cheese *(or Parmesan, if you prefer)*

Meat & Fish

☐	2	Roasting hens, 5-6 lbs each
☐	6 Slices	Bacon

Canned Vegetables, Fruits, & Dried Fruits

☐	2⅓ Cups	Chicken broth
☐	1 (6-oz) Jar	Marinated artichoke hearts

Baking, Spices, & Nuts

☐	1¼ Cups	Sugar
☐	2½ Cups	All-purpose flour
☐	1 tsp	Pure vanilla extract
☐	½ tsp	Nutmeg *(grated fresh whole nutmeg or ground nutmeg)*
☐	1½ tsp	Ground cinnamon
☐	2-3 tsp	Dried Italian seasoning
☐	Dash	Hot sauce
☐		Lemon pepper
☐	½ Cup	Chopped pecans

Condiments

☐	1 Cup	Extra-virgin olive oil
☐	6 Tbsp	Olive oil
☐	½ Cup	Vegetable shortening *(I prefer Crisco)*

Breads

☐	1 Loaf	Italian bread *(or any other sturdy bread)*

Miscellaneous

☐	1 liter	Lemon-lime soda *(to soak apples after slicing)*

Wine & Spirits

☐		Pinot Noir *(recommended wine for meal)*

Autumn Company Dinner

Butternut Bisque

Apple and Romaine Salad

Marinated Pork Tenderloin
with
Apricot Sauce

Herb-Sautéed Vegetables

Our Favorite Carrot Cake

Syrah or Shiraz

I adore fall entertaining! I think it goes back to the whole "theme thing"! There is so much to inspire you—beautiful pumpkins and gourds, the pretty colors and shapes of the fall leaves, and of course a drop in the temperature (much anticipated after a hot Texas summer). It could be that I just love any excuse to have a dinner party—let's celebrate because it's Tuesday!!! I firmly believe that we should make every day an occasion.

Apples are so delicious in the fall, and now we have the luxury of markets offering many choices. I love the tart, crisp Granny Smiths, but you should feel free to experiment with other varieties. The salad for this menu is luscious—blue cheese and apples are a match made in Heaven! Make the dressing a day ahead to shorten your to-do list on the day of the party. The pork tenderloin is best if marinated overnight (making it another entertaining favorite). The sautéed vegetables add a beautiful array of colors and textures to your plate. Be sure all the veggies are cut about the same size so they will cook evenly. Add other favorites, or change the vegetable mix seasonally—this is a delightful side dish.

Carrot cake—YUM! Kevin requires the perfect CIR (cake-icing ratio). This means icing one-fourth as thick as the cake itself. We've found that doubling the frosting satisfies others with similar requests. The cake gets extra coverage, and an auxiliary bowl of frosting to pass around does the trick!

This soup just screams "autumn"! The brilliant orange of the squash makes me think of pumpkins and changing leaves. For an unforgettable presentation, serve this soup in small pumpkins with their tops cut off, seeds removed, and the outsides lightly oiled. Fill with hot soup, replace the lids, place on a baking sheet, and bake 15-20 minutes in a moderate oven. No one makes a prettier serving vessel than Mother Nature!

Butternut Bisque

Serves 8-10 generously

2 lbs	**Butternut squash, peeled, seeded, and cubed**
4 Cups	**Chicken broth**
1 Medium	**Onion, diced**
2 Cloves	**Garlic, minced**
2 Medium	**Russet potatoes, peeled and diced**
3 Large	**Roma tomatoes, peeled, seeded, and diced**
2 Tbsp	**Minced Italian flat-leaf parsley**
1	**Bay leaf** (use dried or fresh)
2 tsp	**Minced fresh thyme** (or ¾ tsp dried thyme leaves)
2 tsp	**Minced fresh marjoram** (or ¾ tsp dried marjoram)
2 Tbsp	**Olive oil**
	Salt and freshly ground black pepper, to taste
1 Cup	**Half & Half** (if desired)
	Crème Fraîche or sour cream to garnish
	Minced Italian flat-leaf parsley to garnish

Combine all ingredients EXCEPT Half & Half in a large stockpot. Add water if needed to cover vegetable mixture. Bring to a boil, reduce heat, and simmer, partially covered, for 30 minutes, until all vegetables are tender. Let cool briefly. Remove bay leaf and discard. Purée the soup mixture in a blender or food processor in batches until coarse or smooth, depending on your preference. Stir in Half & Half for added richness if desired. Taste and adjust seasoning. Reheat soup if necessary and serve. Garnish each serving with a swirl (or a diva crown!) of crème fraîche or sour cream and garnish with additional minced parsley if desired.

Make-Ahead Tip: Prepare the soup a day or two ahead. Cool quickly by placing pot in a sink filled with ice water and stirring frequently. When cool, cover and refrigerate. Place crème fraîche in a squeeze bottle for the garnish. Before serving, reheat soup over low heat, stirring often to prevent scorching.

Fyi... Crème Fraîche

Crème fraîche is a slightly sour and thickened cream with a tangy flavor somewhere between whipping cream and sour cream. It is available in grocery or specialty stores in the dairy case, but is easily made at home. To 1 cup of whipping cream (not ultra-pasteurized), add 2 Tbsp buttermilk. Stir, place in a glass container, cover, and let stand at room temperature for 12 - 24 hours. The mixture will thicken. It is now ready to use. It will keep, covered and refrigerated, for about a week.

How To... Peel and Dice Butternut Squash

Butternut squash is a hard winter squash with a pale tan or cream shell and a sweet orange flesh. It has a cylindrical top and a bulbous base. I find it easiest to handle by first trimming off the top (stem end) and the base (blossom end) with a very sharp, heavy knife or cleaver. Next, I separate the top from the round base. Placing the cut edge on a cutting board, I then cut each piece in half, making a total of 4 pieces. Peel each part using a vegetable peeler with a ceramic or serrated blade. Remove seeds using an ice cream scoop. Place flat edge down on cutting board, cut into uniform slices, then into cubes.

How To ...
Store Oils

Walnut oil is one of the few oils you should store in the refrigerator. Buy in small quantities and use quickly as it can become rancid. Canola oil and olive oil should be stored in a cool, dark pantry.

Apple and Romaine Salad

Serves 6-8

Walnuts:

1½ Cups	**Walnuts** *(halves or coarsely chopped)*
2 Tbsp	**Unsalted butter, melted**
2 tsp	**Sugar**
	Salt and pepper to taste

Vinaigrette:

1	**Granny Smith apple, unpeeled and chopped**
1 Medium	**Shallot, minced**
¼ Cup	**Apple cider vinegar**
1 Tbsp	**Sugar**
1 tsp	**Dry mustard**
	Salt and pepper to taste
⅓ Cup	**Walnut oil**
⅔ Cup	**Canola oil**

Salad:

2	**Ripe apples** *(any type)*, **unpeeled, and thinly sliced**
6 oz	**Crumbled blue cheese or feta cheese**
2 or 3	**Hearts of romaine lettuce, torn into bite-size pieces**

To prepare the walnuts: Preheat oven to 350°. In a bowl, combine walnuts, butter, sugar, salt and pepper. Stir until nuts are coated. Spread out on a baking sheet and bake for 10-12 minutes or until lightly browned. Set aside to cool.

To prepare the vinaigrette: Place all ingredients EXCEPT oils in the bowl of a food processor. Process until combined and apple is pureed. With machine running, add oils in a slow, steady stream. Process until emulsified. Refrigerate to chill before serving. If dressing separates, shake well or reprocess in food processor.

To prepare the salad: Arrange salad greens on a large platter. Top with nuts, apples, and blue cheese. Drizzle with vinaigrette. Serve immediately.

Make-Ahead Tip: The walnuts can be made two days in advance, and the vinaigrette can be prepared a day ahead. Romaine can be washed and torn and stored in a zip-top bag in the refrigerator. Early on the day of serving, apples can be sliced and refrigerated with lemon-lime soda to cover. Drain before using in the salad.

There is no need to worry about bacteria from the raw pork remaining in the marinade you use for the sauce. Boiling the sauce for 3-5 minutes before proceeding is sufficient to kill any microbes. However, to ease your concern, you can always make a separate batch of marinade to use for the sauce.

Buy, Use, and Store Fresh Gingerroot

Gingerroot is a very flavorful knobby root of a tropical plant. It has a thin, tan skin and a pungent, peppery flavor. Peel with a vegetable peeler, and use the pale yellowish flesh. Choose gingerroot that has a smooth and taut appearance and few shriveled areas, which would indicate a lack of moisture. It is a very gnarly root, and it is acceptable to break off the portion you need from a larger piece. Dice, slice or grate to use. Unused portions may be frozen or kept in a jar in the refrigerator covered with dry sherry for up to 3 months. The sherry becomes infused with the flavor and is a nice addition to marinades. Dried ground ginger has a very different flavor from the fresh, and is not usually used interchangeably.

This recipe is a variation of one given to me by my sister, Cherry. The sliced pork tenderloin makes a delicious sandwich on a cocktail roll generously spread with sweet honey Dijon mustard; make extra!

Marinated Pork Tenderloin with Apricot Sauce

Serves 6-8

Pork:

2	Pork tenderloins, about 1 lb each, trimmed of fat and membrane

Marinade:

½ Cup	Soy sauce
½ Cup	Dry sherry
1 Clove	Garlic, minced
2 tsp	Dry mustard
½ tsp	Dried crushed red peppers
1 Tbsp	Minced fresh peeled gingerroot *(or 1 tsp ground dried ginger)*
1 Tbsp	Fresh thyme leaves *(or 1 tsp dried thyme leaves)*
4	Green onions, thinly sliced

Sauce:

	Reserved marinade
1¼ Cups	Apricot preserves
1 Tbsp	Cornstarch
¼ Cup	Cold water
	Additional sliced green onion to garnish

To prepare the pork and marinade: Combine the soy sauce, sherry, garlic, mustard, red peppers, ginger, thyme, and onion in a nonreactive container or a zip-top bag. Add the pork tenderloins. Refrigerate for at least 4 hours or overnight. Remove tenderloins from the marinade *(reserve marinade for later)*. Preheat an outdoor grill until hot. Sear pork on all sides over direct heat. Turn off one side of the grill and move tenderloins so they are no longer over the direct source of heat. Roast, with grill covered, for about 20 minutes, turning once, until done. *(I like my pork tenderloins with a light pink center. I take them off the grill at about 145° internal temperature.)* For indoor preparation, sear pork on a lightly oiled and heated grill pan on the stovetop until browned on all sides. Transfer to a preheated 375° oven for 20 minutes or to the desired degree of doneness. Cover and let rest for 8-10 minutes before slicing.

To prepare the sauce: Place reserved marinade in a small saucepan and boil for 3-5 minutes. Strain through a fine sieve into a clean saucepan. Add apricot preserves and stir until melted. Dissolve cornstarch in water and add to boiling sauce. Continue to cook over medium-high heat; stir until thickened. Serve sliced pork topped with the sauce, and garnish with green onions if desired. It's great served with long grain and wild rice!

Make-Ahead Tip: Two days before the dinner party, marinate the pork tenderloins. One day in advance, sear the tenderloins and refrigerate on a sheet pan; make Apricot Sauce and store in a microwaveable container.

I know you're going to read this and think, "Lemon and horseradish? Yuk!" But I promise it is a delightful combination of flavors and tastes heavenly with this menu. I predict that this will become a favorite side dish.

Herbed Sautéed Vegetables

Serves 6-8

3 Tbsp	**Unsalted butter**
3 Tbsp	**Olive oil**
2 Cloves	**Garlic, finely minced**
¼ Cup	**Minced fresh Italian flat-leaf parsley** (or mixed herbs of your choosing)
	Juice of 2 large lemons
2 Tbsp	**Prepared horseradish** (NOT horseradish sauce or horseradish cream!!)
2 Medium	**Yellow squash, cut into matchsticks**
2 Medium	**Zucchini, cut into matchsticks**
2 Small	**Red bell peppers, cut into matchsticks**
3 Medium	**Carrots, peeled and cut into matchsticks**
	Salt and pepper to taste

In a large nonstick skillet over medium heat, melt the butter with the oil. Add the garlic and parsley and stir for about 30 seconds. Stir in the lemon juice and horseradish. Over medium-high heat, add vegetables to the skillet, toss, and sauté until tender-crisp, about 5 minutes. Serve immediately, seasoned with salt and pepper.

Make-Ahead Tip: One day before, prepare all vegetables, mince garlic and herbs, and juice lemons. Store in refrigerator. Several hours before serving, cook the garlic and the parsley, and add the lemon juice and the horseradish. Remove from heat, cover, and set the skillet aside, finishing the dish immediately before serving.

Our Favorite Carrot Cake

Serves 12

Cake:

2 Cups	All-purpose flour
2 Cups	Sugar
2 tsp	Ground cinnamon
1 tsp	Salt
2 tsp	Baking soda
1 Cup	Canola oil
4 Large	Eggs
3 Cups	Grated peeled carrots (about 3 medium carrots)
1 tsp	Pure vanilla extract

Frosting:

(I always double the frosting, making Kevin a happy man!!)

8 oz	Cream cheese, softened
8 Tbsp	Unsalted butter, softened
1 tsp	Pure vanilla extract
1 lb	Powdered sugar
1-2 Tbsp	Milk (2% or whole)
1 Cup	Chopped toasted pecans (optional)

To prepare the cake: Preheat oven to 350°. Grease and flour two 9-inch cake pans or a 9 x 13-inch cake pan.

In the bowl of an electric mixer, combine the dry ingredients. Add eggs one at a time and beat well on low speed after each. Add in grated carrots and vanilla. Mix until combined. Divide the batter between the round pans or pour into the oblong pan. Bake for about 35 minutes in the round pans or 45-50 minutes in the oblong pan. To test for doneness, a toothpick inserted in the center should come out clean. Remove cake from oven. Let cake rest in the pan on a cooling rack for about 10 minutes, then invert onto the cooling rack, remove pan, and turn back right side up on a second cooling rack to cool completely.

To prepare the frosting: In the bowl of an electric mixer, cream together the cream cheese and the butter until light and fluffy. Add vanilla and combine. Gradually add the powdered sugar, beating well after each addition. Add milk as needed to reach the desired spreadable consistency.

To assemble: If baked in two pans, place first layer top side down on a cake plate. Spread top of layer with about a fourth of the frosting. Top with second layer, right side up. Next frost the sides of the cake, taking care to take the frosting all the way to the top of the cake. Use about two-thirds of the remaining frosting. Frost the top of the cake last. Sprinkle with pecans if using. I usually refrigerate the cake for about an hour to let the frosting set as this makes it much easier to slice. Store any leftover cake in the refrigerator.

Make-Ahead Tip: This cake can be made a day in advance or even made and frozen. Do not uncover it while thawing! Keep the wrap on the cake. This will allow condensation to accumulate on the outside of the plastic wrap rather than on the cake itself.

Culinary Countdown

A Month Before:	Shop for small pumpkins for soup—look in craft stores, grocery stores, and garden centers. Try to get them similar in size (1-cup capacity), with intact, pretty stems.
4 Days Before:	Follow up on RSVPs; verify number of guests.
3 Days Before:	Gather and make ready all table linens, dishes, flatware, glasses, serving utensils, and salt and pepper grinders; plan or order centerpiece; decide on all beverages.
2 Days Before:	Edit grocery list; shop for all items; purchase wines, spirits, and liqueurs.
	Set the table—completely! Remember you'll need a soup spoon and another plate for the pumpkin serving containers!
	Prepare Butternut Bisque. Put crème fraîche in a squeeze bottle.
	Make walnuts for salad; store in zip-top bag.
	Marinate pork tenderloins.
1 Day Before:	Make vinaigrette; refrigerate in a squeeze bottle. Wash salad greens.
	Sear pork tenderloins, transfer to sheet pan, and refrigerate. Make Apricot Sauce and refrigerate in microwaveable container.
	Slice all veggies for sauté; mince herbs and juice lemons. Store in zip-top bags in the refrigerator.
	Make and frost Carrot Cake; store in refrigerator.
Party Day:	**Fall is in the air!**
Early Afternoon:	Slice apples and cover with lemon-lime soda; refrigerate.
	Prepare pumpkins, oil, and place on baking sheet.
	Sauté garlic and parsley for veggies. Add lemon juice and horseradish; set skillet aside.

1 Hour Before:

Remove Bisque from refrigerator and slowly heat.
Preheat oven to 350° for soup.

Remove pork tenderloins from refrigerator to allow them to come to room temperature. Place sauce in microwave.

Cook long grain and wild rice; keep warm.

Remove veggies for sauté from refrigerator.

Put hot soup in pumpkins and bake. Garnish and serve.
Increase oven temperature to 375° for pork tenderloins.

30 Minutes Before:

Remove Carrot Cake from the refrigerator.

Put in pork tenderloins to cook for 20 minutes.

After putting pork in oven, plate the salad and serve.

After clearing salad, remove pork from oven. Heat sauce in microwave. Let tenderloins rest 5-7 minutes. In the meantime, prepare the veggies. Heat skillet on stove for veggies; add veggies and toss to heat and lightly cook through. Slice pork.

Prepare plates. Start coffee.

Serve carrot cake and coffee.

Autumn Company Dinner

For 6-8 people

Produce

☐	2	Ripe apples *(any type)*
☐	1	Granny Smith apple
☐	2 Large	Lemons
☐	2 Medium	Yellow squash
☐	2 Medium	Zucchini
☐	2 lbs	Butternut squash
☐	2 Small	Red bell peppers
☐	6 Medium	Carrots
☐	2 Medium	Russet potatoes
☐	3 Large	Roma tomatoes
☐	2-3	Hearts of Romaine lettuce
☐	5 Cloves	Garlic
☐	1 Medium	Onion
☐	1 Medium	Shallot
☐	8	Green onions
☐	6 Tbsp	Fresh minced Italian flat-leaf parsley
☐	½ Cup	Fresh minced Italian flat-leaf parsley for Butternut Bisque garnish
☐	5 tsp	Fresh minced thyme
☐	2 tsp	Fresh minced marjoram
☐	1 Tbsp	Fresh minced gingerroot *(or 1 tsp dried ground ginger)*

Dairy & Eggs

☐	1¾ Cups	Unsalted butter
☐	1-2 Tbsp	Milk *(2% or whole)*
☐	1 Cup	Half & Half
☐	½ Cup	Crème fraîche or sour cream
☐	4 Large	Eggs

Meat & Fish

☐	2	Pork Tenderloins—about 1 lb each

Cheese & Deli

☐	8 oz	Cream cheese
☐	6 oz	Blue cheese, crumbled *(or feta cheese, if preferred)*

Canned Vegetables, Fruits, & Dried Fruits

- [ ] 4 Cups — Chicken broth

Baking, Spices, & Nuts

- [ ] 2¼ Cups — Sugar
- [ ] 1 lb — Powdered sugar
- [ ] 2 Cups — All-purpose flour
- [ ] 2 tsp — Pure vanilla extract
- [ ] 2 tsp — Baking soda
- [ ] 1 Tbsp — Cornstarch
- [ ] ½ tsp — Dried crushed red peppers
- [ ] 2 tsp — Ground cinnamon
- [ ] 3 tsp — Dry mustard
- [ ] 1 — Bay leaf *(use dry or fresh)*
- [ ] 1½ Cups — Walnuts
- [ ] 1 Cup — Pecans *(optional)*

Condiments

- [ ] 5 Tbsp — Olive oil
- [ ] 1⅔ Cups — Canola oil
- [ ] ⅓ Cup — Walnut oil
- [ ] ¼ Cup — Apple cider vinegar
- [ ] ½ Cup — Soy sauce
- [ ] 2 Tbsp — Prepared horseradish *(not horseradish sauce or cream)*
- [ ] 1¼ Cups — Apricot preserves

Miscellaneous

- [ ] 1 liter — Lemon-lime soda *(to soak sliced apples)*

Wine & Spirits

- [ ] ½ Cup — Dry sherry
- [ ] Syrah or Shiraz *(recommended wines for meal)*

My Best Tex-Mex

Kevin's Margaritas

Kevin's Roasted Salsa

Roasted Corn Soup with Lime Cream

South-of-the-Border Salad
with Cumin Vinaigrette

Green Chile Chicken Enchiladas

Mexican Brownies

Chilean Carmenere

You've gotta have a good Tex-Mex menu under your belt if you entertain in Texas. This one has all the good flavors. Trust me, these recipes have been fine-tuned over many a margarita!! Without a doubt, Kevin's salsa is divine. The depth of flavor comes from roasting the vegetables and toasting the garlic, oregano, and onions. We like to serve it warm with chips. When serving spicy food to your friends, it's better to under-spice than over-spice. You can always have some sliced jalapenos on the side to enhance the fire! We will sometimes prepare margaritas ahead of time; we prefer the frozen type. Pour them into heavy-duty zip-top plastic bags and lay them flat in the freezer. They stay nice and slushy. Don't forget the salt and the slice of lime!

I really enjoy the salad with this menu. It gives nice color to the plate, the fruit offsets the heat, and also keeps the meal from being so starchy. Note that we do not include the traditional refried beans or Mexican rice—the enchiladas are rich enough. A salad is a welcomed accompaniment. But perhaps we're just saving ourselves for dessert. I feel chocolate is a food group unto itself, and a very necessary one to a well-balanced diet. These brownies are, in a word—killer! They are just this side of fudge…the only way you can mess them up is by overcooking them. They are so easy and so, so good…definitely a "keeper" recipe. "OK, I'll have another margarita, please!" Olé!

When I had my catering business in Denver, one of our customers requested these on a regular basis. We delivered them, frozen in baggies, right to our clients' freezer. They lived on a golf course, and we found out later that the lady of the house would just pop a straw into the corner of the baggie, hop in the golf cart, and sip as she drove along!

Kevin's Margaritas

Serves 4-6

1 (12-oz) Can	**Frozen limeade concentrate** *(the higher the quality, the better)*
6 oz	**Tequila** *(or more!)*
2 oz	**Triple Sec** *(or other orange-flavored liqueur)*
¼ Can	**Water**
	Ice to fill blender
	Rimming salt
	Lime slices

Place limeade, tequila, Triple sec, and water in a blender. Fill with ice. Blend until smooth and pour into salt-rimmed glasses. Top with a lime slice. Repeat throughout the evening!

Make-Ahead Tip: Make several days in advance and freeze flat in zip-top bags. The alcohol prevents them from freezing hard, so they are perfect to spoon into a margarita glass!

Tomatillos

The tomatillo is sometimes referred to as the "Mexican green tomato." It's related to the gooseberry, as evidenced by its papery husk. Tomatillos are sold in markets with their husks intact. Before using, remove the husk to reveal the firm green fruit. Be sure to wash well after removing the husk—the fruit is covered with a sticky residue. Tomatillos are tart with a slight lemon taste, and are quite acidic. They can be used raw or cooked.

Don't be put off by the number of ingredients and steps—it is so worth it!

Kevin's Roasted Salsa

Serves a crowd

Oven-roasted Vegetables:

5 Medium	**Tomatoes** *(we prefer Roma tomatoes because they're meaty)*	
5	**Fresh ripe tomatillos, husks removed and washed**	
2	**Fresh jalapeno peppers**	
1	**Fresh habanero pepper** *(optional)*	

Pan-roasted Vegetables:

1 Medium	**Onion, sliced**	
3 Cloves	**Garlic, whole and unpeeled**	
1 tsp	**Dried Mexican oregano**	

Charred Peppers:

5	**Fresh New Mexico- or Big Jim-style green chilies**

Finishing Ingredients:

	Salt and pepper to taste
	Fresh minced cilantro to taste
½ tsp	**Sugar** *(or more as needed to tame the tartness of the tomatillos)*
	Tortilla chips for serving

To prepare oven-roasted vegetables: Preheat oven to 400°. Roast whole tomatoes, tomatillos, jalapenos, and habanero pepper in a shallow pan for about 20 minutes. Remove from oven and set aside. Take vegetables out of the pan and place in a colander over the sink *(if the tomatoes haven't split open during the roasting process, you may want to cut them open with a knife to allow the seeds to drain out)*. The colander allows the watery liquid to drain off, giving a rich texture to your salsa.

To prepare pan-roasted vegetables: As the warm vegetables drain, heat a heavy skillet (cast-iron, if you have it) and pan-roast sliced onion until browned on each side. Remove and place in the bowl of a food processor. In the same skillet, pan-roast unpeeled garlic cloves and oregano. When browned, remove from the pan, peel garlic, and place in food processor bowl with the onion. *(Do not use nonstick skillets for this! Pans for this recipe are not oiled, and heating a nonstick pan while it is empty is not good for the cooking surface!!)*

To prepare charred peppers: Preheat broiler. In another shallow pan, place green chilies, halved lengthwise, cut side down. Broil until outside is blistered and blackened. You can also blacken the peppers on all sides over a gas flame on your stove or out on the grill. Keep the peppers whole and turn them until all sides are very charred. Remove immediately and place in a bowl. Cover with plastic wrap to steam; this will loosen the skin. When cool enough to handle, peel peppers, discarding charred skin and seeds. Place in food processor.

To finish the salsa: Place oven-roasted vegetables in food processor with the pan-roasted ones and the peeled chilies. Pulse until desired consistency is reached. Season with salt, pepper, and cilantro. Add sugar if the mixture is too tart. This salsa is best when served warm. Enjoy with chips and margaritas!

Make-Ahead Tip: Prepare salsa a day in advance. Keep refrigerated. Warm in microwave before serving.

When entertaining, it's such a "Diva thing" to want to go that little extra step other hostesses don't. This soup makes the dinner a bit more special. The flavors are rich and complex, and it adds a visually pretty component to the menu. We garnished with an oven-toasted corn tortilla cut in a cactus shape. How "Martha, Martha"!!

Roasted Corn Soup with Lime Cream

Serves 6

Soup:

6 ears	**Corn, shucked** (or 3¾ cups frozen corn kernels, thawed and drained)	
6 oz	**Spanish chorizo** (the hard, dry type), **diced** (or any dry, spicy sausage)	
4 Tbsp	**Olive oil**	
1 Medium	**Onion, minced**	
2 cloves	**Garlic, minced**	
2½ tsp	**Ground cumin**	
6 Cups	**Chicken broth**	
⅓ Cup	**Yellow cornmeal**	
3 Tbsp	**Minced fresh cilantro**	
	Salt and pepper to taste	

Lime Cream:

4 Large	**Limes, zested and juiced**
1 Cup	**Heavy whipping cream**
½ Cup	**Finely minced cilantro**
	Salt and pepper

To prepare the soup: Cut corn from cobs and reserve the cobs. In a large stockpot over medium-high heat, cook corn kernels and chorizo in oil until the corn is golden brown. This adds depth of flavor to the soup; be patient. Sip a margarita—you'll just *feel* more patient!! Add the onion and the garlic, stir in the cumin, and cook for about 3 minutes longer. Add the chicken broth and corn cobs *(they impart more flavor)* and simmer, covered, for about 30 minutes. Remove and discard the cobs. **Stop here if making soup ahead. See Make-Ahead Tip, page 97.** Whisking constantly, add the cornmeal, and cook until the mixture thickens. Stir in the cilantro and adjust seasonings. Garnish with lime cream before serving

To prepare the Lime Cream: Simmer lime zest, juice, and cream until reduced by half in a medium saucepan over medium heat. Place in bowl of food processor with the cilantro, and process until smooth. Add salt and pepper. Strain through a fine-mesh sieve, discard solids, and place in a squeeze bottle. It can be used warm or cold. Drizzle on top of soup before serving. *(Lime cream is also very yummy drizzled on top of the enchiladas!)*

Make-Ahead Tip: A day in advance, prepare the soup up to the point where you add the cornmeal. Store the soup in the refrigerator. About 20 minutes before serving, slowly heat the soup on the stovetop to a simmer. Continue with the recipe, adding the cornmeal and cilantro, and adjust the seasonings.

Jicama

Jicama is a Mexican root vegetable that is large and bulbous with a thin brown skin that is easily removed with a vegetable peeler. The white flesh is very crunchy, with a sweet, nutty flavor. It reminds me of the taste and texture of water chestnuts. A little squeeze of lime juice on a slice of raw jicama is magical, as is a sprinkle of chili powder. Try it as a snack with an ice-cold beer!

South-of-the-Border Salad with Cumin Vinaigrette

Serves 8

Salad:

¾ Cup	Peeled and chopped jicama
1	Carrot, shredded
¾ Cup	Shredded red cabbage
3	Green onions, thinly sliced
½ Cup	Diced bell pepper (a combination of red and green is nice)
3 Large	Roma tomatoes, diced
1 (11-oz) Can	Mandarin oranges, drained
1 (15-oz) Can	Black beans, rinsed and drained
2	Avocados, diced (optional)
6-8 Cups	Mixed salad greens

Cumin Vinaigrette: Makes about 1 cup

¼ Cup	Apple cider vinegar
1½ tsp	Dijon mustard
1 tsp	Minced fresh oregano
¾ tsp	Ground cumin
1 Clove	Garlic, pressed
½ tsp	Freshly ground black pepper
¼ tsp	Salt
1 Tbsp	Fresh minced cilantro
Dash	Hot sauce
¾ Cup	Canola oil

To prepare the salad: Combine all the ingredients in a large bowl. Toss to distribute evenly. Add enough dressing to coat lightly; toss well. Place on chilled salad plates and serve immediately. Pass additional vinaigrette.

To prepare the vinaigrette: Combine the vinegar, mustard, oregano, cumin, garlic, pepper, salt, cilantro, and hot sauce in a small bowl. Whisk well. Slowly drizzle in the oil, whisking constantly until smooth and emulsified. Dressing can also be made in a food processor. Simply add all ingredients except the oil; pulse to combine. With the machine running, add the oil in a slow, steady stream. Refrigerate for up to one week.

Make-Ahead Tip: Prepare all the salad ingredients (except the avocados) a day in advance and store each separately in zip-top bags in the refrigerator. Make the vinaigrette a day in advance and store in a squeeze bottle or tightly covered container so it can be shaken in the event it separates.

Green Chile Chicken Enchiladas

Serves 6

Sour Cream Filling:

2 Cups	Sour cream
¼ Cup	Milk (2% or whole)
1 tsp	Ground cumin
	Salt and pepper to taste

Green Chile Sauce:

1 (26-oz) Can	Tomatillos, drained
2 Cloves	Garlic, pressed
2 Tbsp	Fresh minced cilantro
	Salt and pepper to taste
2 Tbsp	Olive oil
1 Medium	Onion, chopped
2 (4-oz) Cans	Diced green chilies

Enchiladas:

12	Corn tortillas
2½ Cups	Cooked, diced chicken
¾ Cup	Grated Monterey Jack cheese

Topping:

	Remaining sour cream filling
	Remaining green chile sauce
1¼ Cups	Grated Monterey Jack cheese
	Chili powder to garnish
	Additional cilantro to garnish

To prepare the sour cream filling: In a medium bowl, combine the sour cream, milk, and cumin. Add salt and pepper to taste.

To prepare the green chile sauce: Puree tomatillos, garlic, and cilantro in the bowl of a food processor. Adjust seasonings. Heat oil in a large skillet and sauté the onions and green chilies until the onion is translucent. Remove from heat. Add the tomatillo mixture. Stir to combine.

To assemble the enchiladas: Preheat oven to 350°. Grease a 9 x 13-inch casserole dish. Cover bottom of dish with about ½ Cup of green chile sauce. Soften corn tortillas (to do this, heat a small amount of canola oil in a skillet and dip tortillas in briefly), then fill with some chicken, a couple of spoonfuls of the sour cream mixture, and about a tablespoon of grated cheese. Roll tortillas up, placing seam side down in prepared dish. Repeat with remaining tortillas. Drizzle with remaining sour cream mixture, then top with the remaining green chile sauce, then the grated cheese. Bake for 30-40 minutes or until heated through. Garnish with chili powder and fresh cilantro.

Make-Ahead Tip: Enchiladas may be assembled in the casserole dish a day in advance, covered tightly, and stored in the refrigerator. Remove from refrigerator and uncover about 30 minutes before placing in the oven to heat. You may need to increase cooking time by about 10 minutes to heat completely through before serving.

I serve these at practically every party—a no-brainer to make, and so chocolaty and good. I once had a guest who became distraught when she discovered that the brownies were all gone before she got to them. She announced to me that they were gone; I apologized. There was nothing I could do. She wouldn't let up. She told me about three more times that evening. She was *mad!* The next time I made them, I wrapped up two and gave them to her the minute she walked in the door. I wanted no more of her whining!

Mexican Brownies

Makes 24

1 Cup	**Unsalted butter, melted**
⅓ Cup	**Unsweetened cocoa powder**
2 Cups	**Sugar**
4 Large	**Eggs**
1½ Cups	**All-purpose flour**
1 tsp	**Ground cinnamon**
½ tsp	**Salt**
1 tsp	**Pure vanilla extract**
2 Tbsp	**Kahlúa** (or other coffee-flavored liqueur)
2 Cups	**Semisweet chocolate chips**
1 Cup	**Chopped pecans** (optional)
	Powdered sugar for dusting

Preheat oven to 325°. Grease a 9 x 13-inch baking pan. Make these brownies by hand, not with an electric mixer!! In a large mixing bowl, stir together the melted butter, cocoa powder, and sugar until well blended. Add eggs one at a time and beat well after each addition. Add in flour, cinnamon, salt, vanilla, and coffee-flavored liqueur, and stir until mixture is smooth. Stir in chocolate chips and pecans *(if using)*. Spoon into prepared pan, and smooth the top of the batter. Bake 35 to 40 minutes or until the brownies are pulling away from the sides of the pan. *They will not test done with a toothpick as these are very moist brownies.* Allow to cool completely in pan. Cut into 24 pieces and dust with powdered sugar before serving. Store in an airtight container.

Make-Ahead Tip: Prepare brownies a day in advance, but do not cut. Cover tightly and store at room temperature.

4 Days Before:	Follow up on RSVPs; verify number of guests.
3 Days Before:	Gather and make ready all table linens, dishes, flatware, glasses, serving utensils, and salt and pepper grinders; plan for or order centerpiece;decide on all beverages.
2 Days Before:	Edit grocery list; shop for all items, including wines, spirits, and liqueurs.
	Set the table—completely!
	Make several batches of margaritas; freeze in zip-top bags.
	Prepare Lime Cream for soup; refrigerate in squeeze bottle.
1 Day Before:	Make salsa and refrigerate in a microwave-safe container.
	Prepare soup to stage before adding the cornmeal and cilantro; refrigerate.
	Prepare salad dressing; chop and prepare all salad ingredients except avocados, and store in separate zip-top bags; wash salad greens; store all in refrigerator.
	Prepare and assemble enchiladas. Cover and refrigerate.
	Make the brownies; cover tightly and store at room temperature.
Party Day!	**Prepare to party—Diva style!**
Early Afternoon:	Rim margarita glasses.
	Cut brownies; dust with powdered sugar; put on platter or dessert plates; cover tightly.
1½ Hours Before:	Remove Lime Cream from refrigerator.
	Remove enchiladas from refrigerator to take the chill off; preheat oven to 350°; put in to bake about 45 minutes before serving.
30 Minutes Before:	Transfer frozen margaritas to a pitcher; store in freezer until guests arrive, then fill rimmed glasses and garnish with lime slices.

Warm salsa in microwave; serve with chips.

Heat soup and add cornmeal and cilantro about 30 minutes before serving; keep warm; heat Lime Cream if desired; serve soup.

After soup, assemble salad and serve with enchiladas.

Serve or pass brownies.

My Best Tex-Mex

For 6 people

Produce

☐	6	Limes
☐	2	Avocados
☐	6 Ears	Corn
☐	5 Medium	Tomatoes *(I prefer Roma)*
☐	3 Large	Roma tomatoes
☐	5	Fresh ripe tomatillos
☐	¾ Cup	Chopped jicama
☐	1	Carrot
☐	¾ Cup	Shredded red cabbage
☐	½ Cup	Diced red or green bell pepper *(a combination is nice)*
☐	6-8 Cups	Mixed salad greens
☐	8 Cloves	Garlic
☐	3 Medium	Onions
☐	3	Green onions
☐	2	Fresh jalapeno peppers
☐	1	Fresh habanero pepper *(optional)*
☐	5	Fresh New Mexico- or Big Jim-style green chilies
☐	1½ Cups	Minced fresh cilantro *(more for garnish)*
☐	1 tsp	Minced fresh Mexican oregano
☐	1 tsp	Minced fresh oregano

Dairy & Eggs

☐	1 Cup	Unsalted butter
☐	¼ Cup	Milk *(2% or whole)*
☐	1 Cup	Heavy whipping cream
☐	2 Cups	Sour cream
☐	4 Large	Eggs

Cheese & Deli

☐	2 Cups	Grated Monterey Jack cheese

Meat & Fish

☐	6 oz	Spanish chorizo *(the hard, dry type or any dry, spicy sausage)*
☐	2½ Cups	Cooked, diced chicken

Canned Vegetables, Fruits, & Dried Fruits

☐ 6 Cups   Chicken broth
☐ 1 (11-oz) Can   Mandarin oranges
☐ 1 (15-oz) Can   Black beans
☐ 2 (4-oz) Cans   Diced green chilies
☐ 1 (26-oz) Can   Tomatillos

Baking, Spices, & Nuts

☐ 2 Cups   Sugar
☐   Powdered sugar for dusting brownies
☐ 1½ Cups   All-purpose flour
☐ 1 tsp   Vanilla
☐ ⅓ Cup   Unsweetened cocoa powder
☐ 2 Cups   Semisweet chocolate chips
☐ ⅓ Cup   Yellow cornmeal
☐ 1 tsp   Ground cinnamon
☐ 5 tsp   Ground cumin
☐ 1 tsp   Dried Mexican oregano
☐   Chili powder to garnish enchiladas
☐ 1 Cup   Chopped pecans *(optional for the brownies)*

Condiments

☐ 6 Tbsp   Olive oil
☐ 1 Cup   Canola oil
☐ ¼ Cup   Apple cider vinegar
☐ 1½ tsp   Dijon mustard
☐ Dash   Hot sauce
☐   Rimming salt for margaritas

Breads

☐ 12   Corn tortillas
☐   Tortilla chips to serve with salsa

Freezer

☐ 1 (12-oz) *Can*   Frozen limeade

Wine & Spirits

☐ 6 oz   Tequila *(or more)*
☐ 2 oz   Triple Sec *(or other orange-flavored liqueur)*
☐ 2 Tbsp   Kahlúa *(or other coffee-flavored liqueur)*
☐   Chilean Carmenere *(recommended wine for meal)*

The Husband-Catching Supper

Broccoli Salad

Molly's Brisket

Green Chile Rice

Monte's Chocolate Sheath Cake

Cabernet Sauvignon
or a
Full-Bodied Merlot

Ok, for all you gals out there wanting to catch the man of your dreams, this is the menu for you! I can't begin to count how many times I made this *exact* meal throughout the courtship period with Kevin! (I'm probably *still* paying off charge cards for brisket purchases from Tony's Meats in Denver!) But after the number of briskets consumed, I'm convinced that the way to a man's heart *is* through his stomach.

The Broccoli Salad is so simple—very basic ingredients. I honestly don't know what the magic is, but it is delicious and well received every time I serve it. Nothing is easier to make than this brisket. Be sure to allow the full 6 hours for the meat to become fall-apart tender. The Green Chile Rice is a yummy barbecue accompaniment. The sour cream and cheese is the perfect foil for spicy flavors, and the chile taste is very *Texas*. It is wonderful because it can be assembled the day before, and baked while you are tossing the salad and slicing the brisket.

What man doesn't love chocolate cake? There are zillions of recipes for this type of cake, but I think my mom, Monte, had the best recipe of all! The hint of cinnamon is divine. If you are fortunate enough to have a friend in the pecan business, request the tiny Texas native pecans. They are the very best. I call them "Barbie" pecans…so perfectly shaped and delicious. Annette Rath, co-owner of the Cuero Pecan House, is the best source for pecans! You might even say they are *the icing on the cake!*

This salad became such a favorite of Kevin's that he requested it a bit too often. I finally put my foot down and said, "No more Broccoli Salad!" A couple of weeks later he came over for dinner, and when I opened the door he was standing there with a beautiful head of broccoli wrapped in florist paper with trailing ribbons! I got the hint. He got his salad!

Best Broccoli Salad

Serves 6-8

Salad:

2 Heads	Fresh raw broccoli, cut into small florets *(reserve stems for another use)*
1 Pint	Cherry or grape tomatoes, halved or quartered
8 oz	Sliced button mushrooms
8 oz	Bacon, fried crisp, drained, and crumbled
½ Small	Red onion, thinly sliced or diced
1 Large	Avocado, peeled and diced
	Salt and freshly ground black pepper to taste

Dressing:

1½ Cups	Ranch dressing *(I use Marie's, but pick your favorite)*

To prepare the salad: Combine all salad ingredients in large bowl except for avocado and Ranch dressing.

To serve: This salad isn't good leftover, so dress only the amount to be consumed during this meal! Immediately before serving, add dressing sparingly. Add about half the dressing, toss to coat vegetables, and add more if necessary. Add salt, pepper, and diced avocado. Toss a final time! It's better to underdress (the salad) than overdress...a concept women have known for years!

Make-Ahead Tip: The day before, wash and slice or chop all vegetables except the avocado. Store separately in zip-top bags in the refrigerator. The bacon can be fried and crumbled, but refrigerate.

Ladies, this is it—the recipe to lure the man of your dreams into your clutches and make him yours forever!!! It certainly worked for me!

Molly's Brisket
(Total cooking time: 6 hours)

Serves 8
(or more, depending on size)

1 Whole	*Beef brisket, well trimmed of fat*
	Salt and pepper
	Celery seed
	Worcestershire powder
	Garlic powder
	Onion powder
	Worcestershire sauce
1 box	*Lipton Beefy Onion Soup Mix (2 envelopes)*
1 Large	*Onion, thinly sliced*
8 oz	*Sliced button mushrooms (optional)*
	Your favorite barbecue sauce

To prepare the brisket: Preheat oven to 300°. Use heavy-duty foil; tear two LONG pieces and place them in a cross on a baking sheet with 1-inch sides. Place brisket in the center and season the leanest side *generously* with salt, pepper, celery seed, Worcestershire powder, onion powder, garlic powder, and several dashes of Worcestershire sauce. Turn brisket over, and repeat on the other side with the same seasonings. Remember, season generously! The side with the most fat should be up during cooking. Next, sprinkle the top with the two envelopes of the onion soup mix. Top with sliced onion and mushrooms, if you are using them. Drizzle top with barbecue sauce *(maybe ½ -¾ Cup)*. Wrap tightly in the foil. You want to be sure no juices escape.

Bake in the slow oven 5 hours. At the end of the 5 hours, open foil up to expose the top of the brisket. **Careful!** It's very hot, and steam rushes out as you open the package. Add more barbecue sauce *(about the same amount as before)* and return the brisket, uncovered, to the oven for another hour. The cooking time is always the same, regardless of the size of the brisket.

Remove the brisket from the oven. Carefully transfer it to a cutting board. Tent it with foil to keep it warm and let it rest about 15 minutes for juices to redistribute before slicing. Slice thinly across the grain. I find an electric knife is best for this job!

To prepare the sauce: Pour drippings collected in the foil into a fat separator. Transfer only the defatted drippings to a saucepan, add more barbecue sauce, and thicken as desired with a bit of cornstarch dissolved in cold water.

Make-Ahead Tip: The brisket can be made and sliced the day before. Reheat, covered tightly, at 350° for 20-30 minutes or until hot throughout. It can also be cooked and frozen.

Green Chile Rice

Serves 8-10

Rice:

1½ Cups	Regular long grain rice
3¼ Cups	Water
1 tsp	Salt
1 Tbsp	Unsalted butter

Chile Mixture:

4 Tbsp	Unsalted butter
1 (7-oz) can	Diced green chilies
1 or 2	Fresh jalapeno peppers, **minced** (amount is up to you!)
½ Cup	Diced onion

Additions:

1 Cup	Sour cream
¾ Cup	Grated Monterey Jack cheese (with or without peppers)
¾ Cup	Grated cheddar cheese
	Salt and pepper to taste

Topping:

¼ Cup	Grated Monterey Jack cheese
¾ Cup	Grated cheddar cheese
	Minced fresh parsley or cilantro for garnish

To prepare the rice: Place rice, water, salt, and 1 Tbsp butter in a 3-quart saucepan over medium-high heat. Bring to a boil, reduce heat to simmer, cover, and cook for about 20 minutes or until the liquid has been absorbed.

To prepare the chile mixture: While rice is cooking, melt remaining butter in a small skillet and sauté green chilies, jalapenos, and onion until tender, about 2 or 3 minutes. Stir into warm rice.

Stir in the additions: Mix the sour cream and cheeses into the rice mixture. Taste and correct seasonings.

Topping: Preheat oven to 350°. Butter a 9 X 13-inch baking dish or other baking dish and lightly spoon in rice mixture. Sprinkle with cheeses. Bake uncovered 20-30 minutes or until cheese is melted and mixture is hot throughout. Garnish with parsley or cilantro before serving.

Variation: You can also add ½ -1 tsp ground cumin and about ½ tsp dried oregano if you want, and stir in 1 Tbsp minced cilantro...this perks it up a bit more. The light sour cream works well (nonfat is a no-no...too "plastic"). You can also add cooked diced chicken breast to make a main-dish casserole.

Make-Ahead Tip: The dish can be prepared a day in advance up to the point of being ready to place in the oven. Cover and refrigerate. The day of serving, bake covered for 30 minutes, uncover, and bake for an additional 15 minutes. Garnish with parsley or cilantro before serving.

This is the grand finale! No matter how many helpings of brisket and rice he's had, he will always have room for chocolate cake. If he *doesn't* like chocolate, be immediately suspicious. It's just not normal and you may need to rethink your choice of husband. How sad—and to think you wasted that brisket!

Monte's Chocolate Sheath Cake

Serves 12-15

Cake:

4 Tbsp	Unsweetened cocoa powder
1 Cup	Water
½ Cup	Unsalted butter
½ Cup	Vegetable shortening *(I use Crisco)*
2 Cups	Sugar
2 Cups	All-purpose flour
½ tsp	Salt
1 tsp	Baking soda
1 tsp	Ground cinnamon
2 Large	Eggs, beaten
1 tsp	Pure vanilla extract
½ Cup	Buttermilk

Icing: *(See Note below)*

4 Tbsp	Unsweetened cocoa powder
6 Tbsp	Milk *(2% or whole)*
½ Cup	Butter
1 lb	Powdered sugar
1 tsp	Pure vanilla extract
1 Cup	Coarsely chopped pecans *(optional)*

Vanilla Ice Cream (if desired)

To prepare the cake: Preheat oven to 350°. Grease a 9 x 13-inch cake pan. In a saucepan over medium heat, stir together the cocoa powder, water, butter, and Crisco. Cook and stir until melted and well combined. Mix in the sugar, flour, salt, baking soda, and cinnamon. Mix until smooth. Stir in eggs, vanilla, and buttermilk. Mix well. Pour batter into the prepared pan and bake 30-35 minutes or until a toothpick inserted into the middle of the cake comes out clean. Ice while hot.

To prepare the icing: In a saucepan over medium heat, bring cocoa powder, milk, and butter to a boil. Stir until smooth. Take off heat and stir in powdered sugar and vanilla; mix until smooth. Add chopped pecans. Pour icing over the hot cake and let cool completely. Cut into serving-size portions and enjoy! This cake is great with a scoop of vanilla ice cream!

Note: Because Kevin loves a good CIR *(Cake-Icing-Ratio, meaning the thickness of the icing should be approximately one-fourth the thickness of the cake)*, I usually double the icing!

Make-Ahead Tip: The cake can be made a day in advance and covered tightly. Store at room temperature. (Be sure to hide it from the man in question; he will not wait for the official dinner before sampling.)

Culinary Countdown

In addition to luring your man through your culinary prowess, you must look fabulous. Be sure to allow plenty of fluff and puff time before his arrival!

4 Days Before: Follow up on RSVPs of other guests if you want, but there is only one who really matters, right?

3 Days Before: Gather and make ready all table linens, dishes, flatware, glasses, serving utensils, and salt and pepper grinders; plan or order centerpiece; decide on all beverages.

2 Days Before: Edit grocery list; shop for all items, including wines, spirits, and liqueurs.

Set the table—completely!

1 Day Before: Prepare all salad vegetables except avocado; fry bacon and store in separate zip-top bags in refrigerator.

Cook and slice brisket; refrigerate in pan you will reheat in; make sauce.

Make Green Chile Rice ready for the oven, cover tightly, and refrigerate.

Make the Chocolate Sheath Cake; cover tightly. Store at room temperature.

Get-Your-Man Day! Prepare to make him yours.

Early Afternoon: Cut cake and place on dessert plates; cover tightly.

1½ Hours Before: Remove brisket and sauce from refrigerator.

Remove Green Chile Rice from refrigerator.

1 Hour Before: Preheat oven to 350°.

45 Minutes Before: Put Green Chile Rice in the oven, covered, for 30 minutes; uncover and bake 15 more minutes.

Put brisket in to heat 15 minutes after rice goes in the oven.

Heat sauce for brisket; assemble salad; serve dinner.

Serve cake (wonderful with ice cream).

Repeat meal as needed for desired results.

Husband-Catching Supper

For 8 people

Produce

- [ ] 2 Heads — Fresh raw broccoli
- [ ] 1 Pint — Cherry or grape tomatoes
- [ ] 8 oz — Sliced button mushrooms
- [ ] 8 oz — Sliced button mushrooms *(optional for brisket)*
- [ ] 1 Large — Avocado
- [ ] ½ Small — Red onion
- [ ] 2 — Onions
- [ ] 1 or 2 — Fresh jalapeno peppers
- [ ] ½ Cup — Fresh minced parsley or cilantro

Dairy & Eggs

- [ ] 1½ Cups — Unsalted butter
- [ ] 6 Tbsp — Milk *(2% or whole)*
- [ ] ½ Cup — Buttermilk
- [ ] 1 Cup — Sour cream
- [ ] 2 Large — Eggs

Cheese & Deli

- [ ] 1 Cup — Grated Monterey Jack cheese
- [ ] 1½ Cups — Grated cheddar cheese

Meat & Fish

- [ ] 8 oz — Bacon
- [ ] 1 Whole — Beef brisket

Canned Vegetables, Fruits, & Dried Fruits

- [ ] 1 (7-oz) Can — Diced green chilies
- [ ] 1 Box — Lipton Beefy Onion Soup Mix *(2 envelopes)*

Pasta, Grains, Cereal

☐ 1½ Cups   Regular long grain rice

Baking, Spices, & Nuts

☐ 2 Cups   Sugar
☐ 1 lb   Powdered sugar
☐ 2 Cups   All-purpose flour
☐ 2 tsp   Pure vanilla extract
☐ 8 Tbsp   Unsweetened cocoa powder
☐ 1 tsp   Baking soda
☐ 1 tsp   Ground cinnamon
☐ 1 Cup   Coarsely chopped pecans *(optional for Icing)*
☐   Celery seed
☐   Worcestershire powder
☐   Garlic powder
☐   Onion powder
☐   Worcestershire sauce

Condiments

☐ ½ Cup   Vegetable shortening *(I use Crisco)*
☐ 1½ Cups   Ranch dressing *(I use Marie's but pick your favorite)*
☐ 1½ Cups   Barbecue sauce *(your favorite)*

Wine & Spirits

☐   Cabernet Sauvignon or a Full-Bodied Merlot
            (Recommended wines for meal)

A Diva-licious Luncheon

Shrimp Louis on Asparagus

Curried Chicken and Artichoke Salad

Salad of Roasted Beets and
Panko-Crusted Goat Cheese
with Lemon Vinaigrette

Quick-Rise Dinner Rolls
with Herbed Butter

Elegant Chocolate Mousse
with Raspberry Coulis

Viognier

Every now and then an occasion arises that calls for a lighter meal—not reduced-calorie, necessarily, but not a hot and heavy repast. I love salads and prefer to serve a trio of them rather than one main attraction. The colors and textures are beautiful on the plate, and each provides a special flavor treat for your guests. These are hearty enough for the guys and dainty enough for the gals!

This is the ideal menu for bridal and baby showers, church groups, and civic meetings because everything can be prepared in advance. I've provided ideas for recipe variations—try shrimp instead of chicken in the curried salad; add cooked and diced chicken to the goat cheese and beet salad. Always feel free to take creative liberties with salads. Add in fruits and vegetables that are your favorites or are in season at the market. Change the herbs, vinegars, and oils in the dressings; you will love your creations.

This menu is suitable for a moveable feast if you like to picnic. Serve the goat cheese plain (not Panko-Crusted) and crumbled on top of the salad. Serve rolls at room temperature. Whether at home or in a park, serve this menu very cold and on chilled plates. Entertaining has never been so easy!

Nearly everyone loves shrimp. Be sure to buy large ones for this salad; they're much more impressive. Of course, my favorite is Texas Gulf shrimp!!

Shrimp Louis on Asparagus

Serves 8

How To ...
Cook Asparagus Tender-Crisp

Dressing:

2 Large	Egg yolks
Dash	Tabasco
3 Tbsp	Lemon juice
	Zest of 1 large lemon
2 tsp	Dijon mustard
⅔ Cup	Olive oil
⅔ Cup	Canola oil
2 Tbsp	Prepared horseradish (not horseradish sauce or cream)
3 Tbsp	Chili sauce or cocktail sauce
1 Tbsp	Minced capers, drained and rinsed
2 Tbsp	Minced fresh Italian flat-leaf parsley
	Salt and pepper to taste

Salad:

40 Jumbo	Shrimp (or large), cooked, peeled, and deveined
2 Bunches	Asparagus, trimmed, cooked tender-crisp, and chilled
	Additional parsley to garnish
	Paprika to garnish

Fill a large skillet or sauté pan with water to a depth of about 1½ inches. Bring to a boil. Add a dash of salt and the trimmed asparagus. Be sure all spears are submerged. Cook about 2-3 minutes *(depending on thickness of asparagus)*, test for desired doneness, drain, and immediately place in ice water to stop the cooking. You want to preserve the bright green color. Drain the ice water and pat the asparagus dry. Roll asparagus in paper towels and store in zip-top bags in refrigerator.

To prepare dressing: Place egg yolks, Tabasco, lemon juice and zest, and mustard in the bowl of a food processor. Pulse until combined. With machine running, pour in oils in a slow and steady stream. Continue processing until mixture is emulsified into a smooth mayonnaise. Add horseradish, chile sauce, capers, and parsley. Mix well. Add salt and pepper to taste.

To assemble salad: Pour dressing into large mixing bowl; add cooked shrimp, and stir to coat well. Refrigerate until serving time.

Arrange asparagus decoratively on chilled salad plates and top each plate with 5 shrimp. Garnish with additional minced parsley and sprinkle with paprika. Serve well chilled.

Make-Ahead Tip: Prepare the dressing, shrimp, and asparagus a day in advance. Store separately in refrigerator.

Variation: Add or substitute (16-24 oz) lump crab meat for the shrimp. Add 2 diced hard-cooked eggs to the dressing. Serve in peeled and pitted avocado halves instead of on the asparagus. Garnish with cherry tomatoes.

How To...

Cook Boneless, Skinless Chicken Breast Halves

We want cooked chicken breast to be tasty, moist, and tender. To achieve this desired result, pound breast halves to an even thickness—not scaloppine, but approximately the same thickness to ensure even cooking. Slice the breast into 5 diagonal strips across the grain. In the meantime bring about 2 inches of water or chicken broth to a boil in a large sauté pan. Season with salt, tops of celery, and a bit of lemon and onion if desired. When water boils, add chicken strips. When water returns to a boil, reduce heat to a gentle simmer, and cook chicken uncovered for 10 minutes. Cover, remove from heat, and let sit 10 minutes more. The result is perfectly cooked, moist chicken breast.

I adore the color of this salad—it just "pops" on the plate. Adjust the curry seasoning to suit your personal preference. Any way you spice it will be delicious!

Curried Chicken and Artichoke Salad

Serves 8

Dressing:

1 Cup	Mayonnaise
¼ Cup	Heavy whipping cream
2 Tbsp	Mild or hot curry powder, or to taste
1 tsp	Beau Monde seasoning
Dash	Hot sauce *(optional)*
	Salt and pepper to taste

Salad:

¾ Cup	Regular long grain rice
1½ Cups	Chicken broth
1 Tbsp	Unsalted butter
½ Cup	Sliced green olives with pimiento
1 Cup	Diced celery
1 (6-oz) Can	Whole water chestnuts, drained and chopped *(optional)*
4	Green onions, sliced, including tops
½ Medium	Red bell pepper, diced
½ Medium	Green bell pepper, diced
1 (6-oz) jar	Marinated artichoke hearts, chopped, including marinade
2 Tbsp	Minced fresh Italian flat-leaf parsley or fresh cilantro
4	Boneless, skinless chicken breast halves, cooked, and diced

To prepare the dressing: Combine mayonnaise, cream, curry powder, Beau Monde seasoning, salt, and pepper in a large bowl.

To prepare the salad: Cook rice in chicken broth with butter until liquid is absorbed, about 20 minutes. Cool to room temperature. Add all other salad ingredients and dressing; stir to combine. Refrigerate to chill thoroughly. Flavor improves if refrigerated overnight.

Make-Ahead Tip: This salad is best when prepared a day in advance.

"Beets," you say. "For company?" Now don't turn up your nose until you taste this—it is so delicious, and very pretty, too!

Salad of Roasted Beets and Panko-Crusted Goat Cheese with Lemon Vinaigrette

Serves 8

Panko-Crusted Goat Cheese:

8 Slices	Goat cheese (from a log, sliced about ⅜" thick), **chilled**
1 Large	Egg white, beaten
1 Cup	Panko crumbs
	Olive oil

Roasted Beets:

3 Large	Red beets (all of similar size)
3-4 Large	Golden beets (all of similar size)

Lemon Vinaigrette:

2 Tbsp	Lemon juice
2 Tbsp	Tarragon wine vinegar
1 Tbsp	Honey
1 Tbsp	Lemon zest
1 Clove	Garlic, minced
¾ Cup	Extra-virgin olive oil
1 Tbsp	Finely minced Italian flat-leaf parsley
	Salt and pepper

Salad:

6-8 Cups	Mixed spring greens
	Toasted chopped walnuts or pecans for garnish

To prepare the goat cheese: Dip rounds of chilled goat cheese gently into beaten egg white, then into the panko crumbs to coat completely. Take care not to let the rounds break!! Transfer to a parchment-lined sheet pan and return to the refrigerator to chill thoroughly. Heat a small amount of olive oil in a nonstick skillet or sauté pan. Add goat cheese rounds and cook until light golden brown, then turn and brown the second side. Place on top of salad while still warm. Note: Dental floss is perfect for neatly slicing the goat cheese.

To prepare the beets: Scrub beets and cut off greens to within an inch of the beet. Wrap red beets together in a sheet of heavy-duty foil; wrap golden beets together in another foil packet. Place on a baking sheet and bake at 375° for 45 minutes to an hour, or until beets are tender when pierced with a wooden skewer. When cool enough to handle, peel the beets and dice into half-inch cubes. *I recommend wearing plastic gloves when working with the beets; they stain EVERYTHING they touch!* Store separately in zip-top bags in the refrigerator until needed.

Panko Crumbs

Panko crumbs are irregularly shaped, coarse, Japanese-style bread crumbs. They create an exceptionally crispy crust. They are usually found with the Asian ingredients at the grocery store; sometimes they are found with other packaged bread crumbs on the baking aisle. Use them for breading fish to sauté or fry, or for anything calling for a bread crumb crust. I love cooking with them!

To prepare the vinaigrette: Combine the lemon juice, vinegar, honey, and lemon zest in the bowl of a food processor. While the machine is running, slowly add the oil in a steady stream. Stir in parsley, salt, and pepper.

To assemble the salad: Toss greens with enough dressing to coat, reserving a bit to drizzle over the top. Top greens with beets, drizzle with remaining dressing, top with warm goat cheese rounds and sprinkle with toasted chopped nuts. Serve immediately.

Make-Ahead Tip: Goat cheese can be prepared and browned a day in advance and refrigerated on a sheet pan until it is rewarmed. Beets and vinaigrette can be prepared a day in advance and stored in the refrigerator. Nuts can be toasted a day or two in advance.

The Rising Bread

Bread rises best in a warm, draft-free area. Conveniently, this may be on top of a refrigerator, in the laundry room on top of the washer or dryer, or on top of a gas range, taking advantage of a lit pilot light. You may, however, need to create a warm environment. Preheat your oven to its lowest setting (usually around 135˚). Turn the oven off and place the rolls or dough inside. This technique works beautifully. Also, heating a bowl of water to boiling in your microwave, removing it, and placing the bowl of bread dough inside the warm, moist cavity will work. Lastly, if time is not critical, dough will rise very slowly if placed in the refrigerator overnight.

What is better than the aroma of freshly baked bread? These rolls are quick to make since they require only one rise. You'll impress your guests with your baking talent!

Quick-Rise Dinner Rolls with Herbed Butter

Makes 24

Rolls:

1 Tbsp	Active dry yeast
½ Cup	Warm water (105˚-115˚)
¼ Cup	Sugar
1 tsp	Salt
1 Cup	Milk (2% or whole), **warmed to 105˚-115˚**
4 Tbsp	Unsalted butter, softened
2 Tbsp	Minced fresh herbs: parsley, thyme, basil, rosemary, or a combination (optional)
3 - 4 Cups	All-purpose flour

Herbed Butter:

Makes 1 Cup

1 Cup	Unsalted butter, softened
¾ tsp	Salt
1 Clove	Garlic, pressed (optional)
6 Tbsp	Finely minced fresh herbs

To prepare rolls: In a small bowl or measuring cup, combine the yeast, warm water, and a pinch of the sugar. Stir and allow to rest until mixture begins to foam and bubble. If nothing has happened in 10 minutes, discard it and begin again, checking the date on the yeast. After mixture begins to bubble, add remaining sugar and salt. Add warm milk and butter to yeast mixture. Beat in herbs *(if using)* and flour, adding the flour in increments to make a soft, but not sticky, dough. Turn out on a lightly floured surface. Knead until smooth and elastic. Shape into 24 balls. Place rolls 2 inches apart on parchment paper or Silpat-lined baking sheets, or greased baking sheets. Lightly cover and let rise in a warm, draft-free area until doubled, about 45 minutes. Preheat oven to 400° and bake rolls for 8-10 minutes until golden brown.

To prepare the herbed butter: Mix together all ingredients in the bowl of a food processor. Roll into a cylinder on waxed paper or plastic wrap or spread in butter molds. Refrigerate until serving time.

Variations: Substitute 1 cup of whole wheat flour for 1 cup of the all-purpose flour. For a Mediterranean flavor, add 2 tablespoons of finely minced oil-packed, sun-dried tomatoes, and 2 tablespoons chopped kalamata olives at the time you add the herbs. Use parsley, rosemary, and basil for the herbs.

How Much Flour for Bread Making?

There are many variables that determine the quantity of flour to be used in a recipe—the humidity of the day, the accuracy of the liquid measurements, the amount of gluten in the flour, and the flour itself. When making bread, you're looking more for a texture than a specific amount of flour. A soft but not sticky dough is desired. Add the flour in small increments, thoroughly incorporating the previous addition before adding more. When the dough begins "cleaning" (begins to come cleanly away from) the sides of the mixing bowl, it is getting close to the proper texture. Check often by touching it. It should feel soft, maybe slightly tacky, but shouldn't cling in a glob to your finger. Knead the dough on a lightly floured surface. The addition of too much flour can make the finished product tough.

Make-Ahead Tip: Make and bake rolls several days, or weeks, in advance and freeze in a zip-top bag. Allow to defrost in the unopened bag so condensation will form on the outside of the bag, not on the surface of the rolls. Place rolls on a baking sheet and heat at 350° for 5-6 minutes before serving. Herbed butter can be made and frozen weeks in advance.

It's very easy to make the lacy chocolate cup we show in the photo. Inflate a small latex balloon and tie to close. Melt about 2 Cups semisweet chocolate chips with 1 tsp vegetable shortening. Dip the smooth end of the balloon into the chocolate to make a solid "base." Invert balloon in a ramekin so the chocolate side is up. Allow to cool and harden. Rewarm remaining chocolate if necessary and spoon into a pastry bag fitted with a writing tip. Thickly squiggle melted chocolate, connecting to the base and creating the desired shape, size, and depth of bowl. Invert on ramekin and let harden. On waxed paper or parchment paper, pipe a solid disc of chocolate about 3 inches in diameter. Allow the disc to harden. Very carefully cut a tiny hole in the top of the balloon where it is tied. Very slowly let the air out, and ease it away from the chocolate "bowl." Connect the base of the bowl to the chocolate disc with another dab of melted chocolate. Easy!!!

Elegant Chocolate Mousse with Raspberry Coulis

Serves 8-10

Chocolate Mousse:

1½ Cups	**Sugar**
¾ Cup	**Unsweetened cocoa powder**
12 oz	**Cream cheese, softened to room temperature**
2 tsp	**Pure vanilla extract**
1 Tbsp	**Kahlúa** *(or other coffee-flavored liqueur)*
2¼ Cups	**Heavy whipping cream**

Raspberry Coulis:

16 oz	**Frozen raspberries, thawed** *(or fresh)*
	Sugar to taste
½ Cup	**Water**
1 Tbsp	**Cornstarch dissolved in ¼ cup cold water, if needed**

To Serve:

Chocolate cups
Shaved chocolate to garnish
Pirouette cookies to garnish
Fresh raspberries to garnish
Fresh mint sprigs to garnish

To prepare the mousse: In a small bowl, stir the sugar and cocoa powder together. This helps to evenly distribute the cocoa powder. Using an electric mixer, beat the softened cream cheese, sugar, cocoa, vanilla, and Kahlúa until smooth. Beat about 4 minutes more until light and fluffy. In another bowl, beat the whipping cream until stiff. Stir about a third of the whipped cream into the chocolate mixture to lighten it, then gently fold in the remaining whipped cream. Cover and refrigerate until well chilled.

To prepare the Raspberry Coulis: Purée the thawed berries, with any juices, in a food processor. Pour into a saucepan and add sugar and water. Bring to a boil and simmer 5-7 minutes. Strain through a fine-mesh sieve, pressing hard on solids but removing the seeds. Place the liquid back into the saucepan and thicken as desired with cornstarch dissolved in cold water (bringing mixture to a full, rolling boil). Chill sauce before serving.

To assemble and serve: Transfer to a pastry bag fitted with a large star tip and pipe into purchased chocolate cups or serving dishes. Stemmed goblets are pretty! Garnish with shaved chocolate and a cookie; serve chilled, in a puddle of Raspberry Coulis.

Variation: Experiment with different liqueurs in the mousse—Amaretto (almond-flavored), Kirsch (cherry-flavored), Chambord (raspberry-flavored), or Grand Marnier (orange-flavored) all make nice alternatives. Substitute strawberries for the raspberries in the coulis and the garnish.

Make-Ahead Tip: The mousse can be made a day in advance and refrigerated. It can be piped into the individual serving dishes early on the day of the party. Raspberry Coulis can be made a day in advance and refrigerated in a squeeze bottle.

Culinary Countdown

One Month Before: Make and bake rolls; cool completely and freeze. Prepare herbed butter and freeze.

4 Days Before: Follow up on RSVPs; verify number of guests.

3 Days Before: Gather and make ready all table linens, dishes, flatware, glasses, serving utensils, and salt and pepper grinders; plan or order centerpiece; decide on all beverages.

2 Days Before: Edit grocery list; shop for all items EXCEPT shrimp; purchase wines, spirits and liqueurs.

Set the table—completely. Remember a bread basket and linen as well as tongs for the rolls...butter knives too, if you have them!

Toast nuts for the beet salad garnish; store in a zip-top bag.

1 Day Before: Purchase and cook shrimp for Shrimp Louis. Prepare asparagus and make the dressing. Refrigerate all.

Prepare the Curried Chicken and Artichoke Salad; refrigerate overnight for best flavor.

Prepare and brown the goat cheese slices. Refrigerate on a parchment-lined baking sheet, covered, so it is ready to warm before serving. Roast, peel, and dice beets. Refrigerate separately in zip-top bags. Prepare vinaigrette; refrigerate.
Wash salad greens and refrigerate.

Transfer rolls and butter from the freezer to the refrigerator to allow them to thaw.

Prepare the Chocolate Mousse, then chill it. Make the Raspberry Coulis and store in the refrigerator in a squeeze bottle. Wash mint sprigs, spin them dry in a salad spinner, and wrap in a damp paper towel. Place in a zip-top bag, and refrigerate.

Party Day! **Sound the trumpets~the Guys and Gals will soon arrive!**

2 Hours Before: Plate the Shrimp Louis, and the Curried Chicken and Artichoke Salad; refrigerate plates until serving time.

Place rolls on baking sheet; put butter on butter plates on the table.

Pipe Chocolate Mousse into chocolate cups or serving dishes; decorate with Coulis and return to refrigerator.

30 Minutes Before: Preheat oven to 350° for rolls and goat cheese rounds. Heat when ready; transfer rolls to a bread basket; place goat cheese on salad.

Finish the Beet Salad while rolls and goat cheese are warming.

Brew coffee.

After clearing table, garnish dessert and serve.

Ahhhh…It's so good to be the Diva!

A Diva-licious Luncheon

For 8 Guests

Produce

☐	2	Lemons
☐	16 oz	Fresh raspberries *(or frozen raspberries, thawed)*
☐		Additional raspberries to garnish dessert
☐	1 Cup	Diced celery
☐	2 Bunches	Asparagus
☐	4	Green onions
☐	3 Large	Red beets *(all of similar size)*
☐	3-4 Large	Golden beets *(all of similar size)*
☐	2 Cloves	Garlic
☐	6-8 Cups	Mixed spring greens
☐	1	Red bell pepper
☐	1	Green bell pepper
☐	5 Tbsp	Fresh minced Italian flat-leaf parsley
☐	8 Tbsp	Fresh minced herbs: parsley, thyme, basil, rosemary, or a combination *(optional)*
☐		Fresh mint sprigs for dessert garnish
☐		Parsley to garnish Shrimp Louis

Dairy & Eggs

☐	1½ Cups	Unsalted butter
☐	2½ Cups	Heavy whipping cream
☐	1 Cup	Milk *(2% or whole)*
☐	3 Large	Eggs

Cheese & Deli

☐	12 oz	Cream cheese
☐	8 Slices	Goat cheese *(from a log, sliced about ⅜" thick)*

Meat & Fish

☐	4	Boneless, skinless chicken breast halves
☐	40 Jumbo	Shrimp *(or large)*, cooked, peeled, and deveined

Canned Vegetables, Fruits, & Dried Fruits

☐	1½ Cups	Chicken broth
☐	1 (6-oz) Jar	Marinated artichoke hearts
☐	1 (6-oz) Can	Whole water chestnuts

Pasta, Grains, Cereal
☐ ¾ Cup   Regular long grain rice

Baking, Spices, & Nuts
☐ 1¾ Cups   Sugar
☐ 1 Tbsp   Honey
☐ 2 tsp   Vanilla
☐ 3-4 Cups   All-purpose flour
☐ ¾ Cup   Unsweetened cocoa powder
☐ 1 Cup   Panko crumbs
☐ 1 Tbsp   Active dry yeast
☐ 2 Tbsp   Curry powder *(mild or hot)*
☐ 1 tsp   Beau Monde seasoning
☐   Chopped walnuts or pecans to garnish salad

Condiments
☐ ¾ Cup   Extra virgin olive oil
☐ ⅔ Cup   Olive oil
☐ ⅔ Cup   Canola oil
☐ 2 Tbsp   Prepared horseradish *(not horseradish sauce or cream)*
☐ 3 Tbsp   Chili sauce or cocktail sauce
☐ 1 Cup   Mayonnaise
☐ 1 Tbsp   Minced capers
☐ ½ Cup   Sliced green olives with pimiento
☐ 2 tsp   Dijon mustard
☐ 2 Tbsp   Tarragon wine vinegar
☐ 2 Dashes   Hot sauce
☐   Paprika to garnish

Wine & Spirits
☐ 1 Tbsp   Kahlúa *(or other coffee-flavored liqueur)*
☐   Viognier *(recommended wine for meal)*

Miscellaneous
☐   Chocolate cups
☐   Pirouette cookies to garnish dessert
☐   Shaved chocolate to garnish dessert

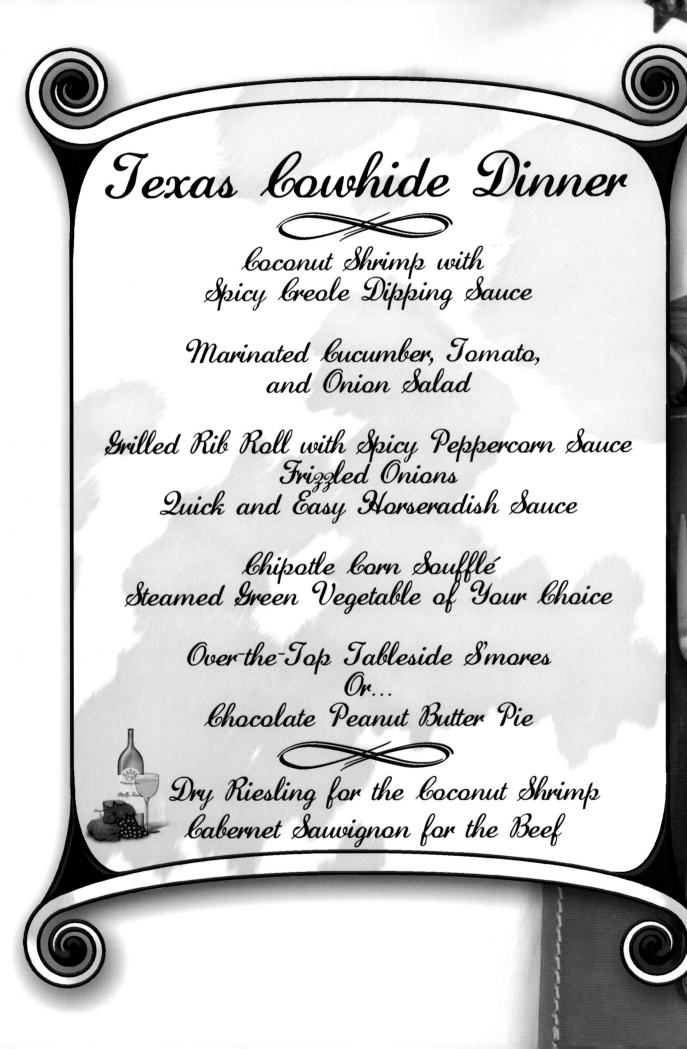

Texas Cowhide Dinner

Coconut Shrimp with
Spicy Creole Dipping Sauce

Marinated Cucumber, Tomato,
and Onion Salad

Grilled Rib Roll with Spicy Peppercorn Sauce
Frizzled Onions
Quick and Easy Horseradish Sauce

Chipotle Corn Soufflé
Steamed Green Vegetable of Your Choice

Over-the-Top Tableside S'mores
Or...
Chocolate Peanut Butter Pie

Dry Riesling for the Coconut Shrimp
Cabernet Sauvignon for the Beef

This was truly the party that took on a life of its own. I was left with a bit of time on my hands between cooking classes in Cuero, Texas. It's a great small town, with interesting antique stores, boutiques, and hardware stores. So what's a girl to do? Shop, of course! I wandered and looked and found a magnificent, HUGE cowhide in one of the stores. I was drawn to it; it practically called my name. As if possessed by a higher force, I bought it (and spent way too much money for it!). I had a vision of the hide as a tablecloth for a Western-style dinner.

And so it went…I hid it from Kevin, believing he'd surely think I'd lost my mind. I thought about the party night and day. I needed leather place mats; the search was on. I found them; I hid them in the closet. My regular white dishes didn't fit the theme; I bought new "Western" ones, and hid those too, of course. Then came the flatware, the napkin rings…and then there were the most adorable individual cast-iron skillets. I had to find special leather coasters—you couldn't put a hot skillet directly on a plate, now, could you? As the décor grew more grandiose, so did the menu and my wardrobe plans. I found myself with a pink cowboy hat, complete with rhinestone tiara, and pink cowboy boots! They were the only pair, so yes, Cinderella, those boots were gonna fit! They kill my feet, but they look really cute! And when all was said and done, Kevin didn't mind a bit…and had a great time. Here's what we had at this wild and crazy "Texas Cowhide Party"…

You're gonna love this recipe, and your friends are gonna love you! These tasty morsels have always been a huge hit! Keep this in mind as an appetizer for your next cocktail party.

Coconut Shrimp with Spicy Creole Dipping Sauce

Makes 48

48 Large — Raw shrimp, peeled leaviing the tail on, deveined

Flour Mixture:
½ Cup — All-purpose flour
2 tsp — Cajun seasoning

Batter Mixture:
2 Large — Eggs, beaten
2 tsp — Cajun seasoning
1½ Cups — All-purpose flour
1 Cup — Dark, full-bodied beer (such as Shiner Bock)
1 Tbsp — Baking powder

Coconut for Coating:
3½ Cups — Sweetened flaked coconut

Creole Sauce:
1 Cup — Orange marmalade
1 Cup — Apricot preserves
¼ Cup — Spicy brown mustard
2 Tbsp — Prepared horseradish (not horseradish sauce or cream)

To prepare flour mixture: Combine flour and seasoning mix in a shallow bowl or zip-top bag.

To prepare beer batter: In another bowl, combine eggs, seasoning, flour, beer, and baking powder.

To prepare coconut for coating: Place coconut in a large shallow bowl.

To assemble: Rinse shrimp and toss them in the flour mixture to coat. Dip in batter, roll in coconut, and set aside on a parchment-lined baking sheet. Refrigerate.

To fry: In a deep saucepan or fryer, heat oil to 350°. Fry a few shrimp at a time until golden brown. They need to get dark brown to ensure the batter is fully cooked—test a couple to gauge cooking time. Drain on a cake-cooling rack over a baking sheet lined with paper towels. Keep warm in oven until serving time.

To prepare dipping sauce: Stir together all sauce ingredients; refrigerate until serving time. Serve with warm shrimp.

Make-Ahead Tip: Coat the shrimp early in the day and refrigerate on a sheet pan. Fry the shrimp, then drain them on a cooling rack over a paper towel-lined baking sheet. Let cool, then refrigerate. Reheat on the rack at 350° for 5-7 minutes before serving. Sauce can be made two or three days in advance and refrigerated.

After the rich appetizer of Coconut Shrimp, this salad is a nice, light treat for your palate. Experiment with the flavors—try different vinegars, add some hot peppers, increase or decrease the sugar. Serve it well chilled.

Marinated Cucumber, Tomato, and Onion Salad

Serves 8

Salad:

6 Medium	*Vine-ripened tomatoes, sliced into wedges*
2	*English cucumbers, peeled and sliced into ¼" slices*
¼ Medium	*Red onion, sliced into thin, partial rings or strips*

Marinade:

2 Tbsp	*Water*
½ Cup	*Apple cider vinegar*
1 Tbsp	*Sugar, or to taste*
6 Tbsp	*Olive oil*
	Salt and pepper to taste

To prepare the salad: Place all the vegetables into a non-reactive container or a zip-top bag.

To prepare the marinade: Whisk all ingredients together until sugar dissolves. Pour over vegetables, seal bag, and refrigerate several hours or overnight.

Variation: Add ½ Cup pitted green olives and/or kalamata olives while marinating, then top with 4 oz. crumbled feta cheese before serving.

Make-Ahead Tip: Salad can be made a day in advance and refrigerated overnight.

English Cucumbers

English (sometimes called *hothouse*) cucumbers are found in the grocery store, wrapped in cellophane to prevent moisture loss. They have a nice mild flavor, are almost seedless, and have a very thin skin that does not have to be removed before eating. If they are not available, use a regular cucumber, but be sure to remove the often woody and bitter seeds with a melon baller.

These are absolutely addictive! I made them for a class once, and none of them made it to the steaks. Students kept eating them as fast as I could take them from the fryer. If you like the average onion ring, you'd better double this recipe!

Frizzled Onions
(optional garnish for steaks)

Serves 8 as Garnish

Batter:

1½ Cups	All-purpose flour
1 Tbsp	Cajun Seasoning
1 Large	Egg, beaten
12 oz	Dark, full-bodied beer *(such as Shiner Bock)*

Onions:

1 Large	Onion, very thinly sliced into rings *(use a mandoline if you have one)*
	Flour for dredging onion
	Canola oil for frying
	Sea salt

Heat oil in deep fryer to 375°.

To prepare the batter: Mix all batter ingredients in a large bowl until completely smooth.

To prepare onions: Dredge onion slices in flour. Dip into batter and fry in hot oil until browned and crispy. Drain on cooling rack placed over a paper towel-lined baking sheet and sprinkle with salt. Keep warm in oven until serving time. Pile on top of beef slices that have been drizzled or coated with sauce.

Make-Ahead Tip: Fry onions early in the afternoon. Let drain as directed above. After they cool, refrigerate on the cooling rack. Heat the onions, uncovered, on the cooling rack in a hot oven for a few minutes before serving. This will crisp them up.

Texans love their beef! This is cooked to perfection and has a very flavorful sauce with a little zip from the green peppercorns. It will show your guests that this isn't your first rodeo!

Grilled Rib Roll with Spicy Peppercorn Sauce

Serves 8-10 hungry guests

6-8 lb	Boneless beef rib roll
	Salt, pepper, and garlic salt
	Canola oil for searing

Peppercorn Sauce:

4 Tbsp	Unsalted butter
16 oz	Sliced button mushrooms
3 Cloves	Garlic, minced
½ Cup	Diced red onion
2 Cups	Dry red wine *(reduced as instructed below)*
½ Cup	Green peppercorns *(from a jar, drained of the brine)*
1¼ Cups	Beef broth
¼ Cup	Brown sugar
2 tsp	Dijon mustard
1 tsp	Hot sauce
½ Cup	Worcestershire sauce *(yes, it really is ½ Cup)*
1 Cup	Heavy whipping cream
¼ Cup	Balsamic vinegar
2 Tbsp	Minced fresh Italian flat-leaf parsley
	Salt and pepper to taste
1 Tbsp	Cornstarch dissolved in ¼ cup cold water *(if needed)*

To prepare the rib roll: Trim off excess fat but leave a thin layer to baste the meat as it roasts. Season very generously on all sides with salt, pepper, and garlic salt. Preheat oven to 425°. In a ridged grill pan, large sauté pan, or shallow roaster, heat a small amount of oil until hot. Add beef, fat side down, and sear until browned. Turn and sear the other side. Transfer to the oven and roast for about 1 hour 15 minutes, or until the internal temperature has reached your desired degree of doneness. We like it medium rare, so we remove it at about 135°. We tent it with foil and the temperature increases by 7 to 10 degrees. Let the meat rest for at least 15 minutes to allow juices to redistribute before carving. Slice into nice, thick steaks.

To prepare the sauce: Heat the butter in a large sauté pan until melted and foamy. Add mushrooms, garlic, and red onion. Sauté until onion is tender and mushrooms release their liquid and begin to brown. While this mixture is cooking, reduce wine to ¼ Cup in a small saucepan on medium heat. Add reduced wine to the sauté pan with the mushrooms, then add the beef broth. Simmer uncovered until the mixture is reduced by about a third. Add remaining ingredients and simmer about 20 minutes. Thicken if desired with a bit of the cornstarch dissolved in cold water. Drizzle over the steaks. Top with Frizzled Onions if desired.

Make-Ahead Tip: Prepare sauce a day in advance. Store in refrigerator.

Many of our beef-eating friends love to have a horseradish sauce to enjoy with their beef. This one is super-easy to make, keeps for a week in the refrigerator, and is good on other foods as well. Plus, you're the ultimate host or hostess when you offer a variety of sauces to your guests.

Quick and Easy Horseradish Sauce

(This is a bonus recipe—no photo, but a really tasty sauce for beef)

Makes 1¼ Cups

½ Cup	Mayonnaise
½ Cup	Sour cream
4 Tbsp	Prepared horseradish (not horseradish cream)
3 Tbsp	Minced chives
	Salt and pepper to taste

For sauce: Mix ingredients together and adjust seasoning to taste. Delicious on beef, baked potatoes, and fried fish. Store in refrigerator for up to one week.

Make-Ahead Tip: Prepare up to one week in advance. Store in the refrigerator.

This Texas version of corn pudding gets rave reviews every time. It's very flavorful, taking spice and a smoky flavor from the chipotle peppers. I've even used it as a side dish for brunch!

Chipotle Corn Soufflé

Serves 8-10

1¼ Cups	All-purpose flour
¼ Cup	Sugar
2½ Tbsp	Baking powder
½ tsp	Salt
½ tsp	Cayenne pepper
½ tsp	Ground cumin
¾ Cup	Grated cheddar cheese
2 Tbsp	Minced fresh cilantro
6	Eggs, separated
½ Cup	Unsalted butter, melted
½ Cup	Heavy whipping cream
1 Cup	Cream-style corn
1 (4-oz) Can	Diced green chilies
2	Chipotle peppers *(in adobo sauce),* **minced**
½ Cup	Minced onion
2 Cups	Corn kernels *(fresh, or frozen and thawed)*
½ Cup	Grated cheddar cheese *(to sprinkle on top before baking)*
	Cilantro or parsley to garnish

Preheat oven to 350°. Butter a 9 x 13-inch casserole dish and set aside. Stir together the flour, sugar, baking powder, salt, cayenne, cumin and cheddar cheese. In a separate bowl, mix together the egg yolks, butter, whipping cream, cream-style corn, green chilies, and chipotle peppers. Stir into the dry mixture. Add in the onion and the corn. Beat egg whites until stiff but not dry, and fold into the mixture. Spoon into the prepared pan, top with additional cheddar cheese, and bake 30-40 minutes or until top is golden and mixture is set *(a toothpick inserted in the center will come out clean).* Serve hot, garnished with cilantro or parsley.

Make-Ahead Tip: This dish can be baked a day in advance, refrigerated, and reheated, covered, for 20-30 minutes before serving.

Chipotle Peppers

Chipotle peppers are dried and smoked red-ripened jalapeno peppers. They have a very distinctive smoky, sweet, hot chile flavor. They are most commonly found canned in adobo sauce, a tomato-vinegar-onion mixture. Try them as an addition to stews, sauces, guacamole, or chile con queso. Remember, they are quite spicy! When in doubt, use conservatively.

Create Corn Husk Containers for Chipotle Corn Soufflé

To make the presentation shown in the photo, soak dried corn husks (purchased in Hispanic markets or the produce section of some grocery stores) in hot water until pliable, about 30 minutes. For each cup, overlap the wide ends of 2 husks and press them down into buttered jumbo muffin pans. If needed, hold in place with ramekins. Tie the ends that extend outside the cups with a thin strip of corn husk. Fill each husk-lined cup two-thirds full with batter and bake 15-20 minutes at 350°.

How To ...

Make Nuts Pretty for Toppings

When chopping nuts, you will always get what I call "nut dust" – that fine, dusty residue that accumulates along with the nut pieces, on your cutting board. You do not want this sprinkled across the top of your dessert!! Place the chopped nuts in a fine-mesh sieve and shake over the sink to remove "nut dust". Beautiful, clean nuts remain for sprinkling!

This was so silly, but so much fun! I bought the individual tabletop hibachis from a restaurant supply store, and used fondue forks to skewer the marshmallows. Add a little gel fuel, ignite, and you're around the old campfire! Who knew adults would have such a good time? It was *not* followed by ghost stories (or was it??)!

Over-the-Top Tableside S'mores

Serves 8

32	**Graham cracker squares** *(2½" by 2½")*
3 (3-oz)	**Gourmet chocolate bars, broken into squares**
16 Large	**Marshmallows** *(more if cooking in ramekins)*

For each guest, arrange 4 graham cracker squares, 4 chocolate squares, and 2 or three marshmallows on a plate. No formality...give each guest a fondue skewer and a hibachi, and let them get to work! Toast the marshmallow, place chocolate on the graham cracker, and sandwich together! Messy, but delicious.

If you do NOT have the hibachis, you can still play. Distribute the graham crackers and chocolate as above. Place each guest's marshmallows in shallow ramekins (the type used for crème brûlée). Preheat broiler, place ramekins on a sheet pan and place under the broiler until marshmallows get toasty and soft. Serve the hot marshmallows to each guest, providing them with table knives to spread the warm marshmallow on the crackers. Still fun!

Or...

We've provided a more traditional dessert on the following page. This is what you would get if you crossed a Reese's Peanut Butter Cup with a Three Musketeers—yum!
And not a calorie in it—yeah, right!

Chocolate Peanut Butter Pie

Serves 12-16

Crust:

1½ Cups	**Crushed Oreo-type cookies** *(about 24 whole cookies)*	
¾ tsp	**Ground cinnamon**	
1 Tbsp	**Smooth peanut butter**	
3 Tbsp	**Unsalted butter, melted**	

Filling:

4 oz	**Cream cheese, softened**
¾ Cup	**Powdered sugar**
1 Cup	**Smooth peanut butter**
2 Tbsp	**Heavy whipping cream**
1 tsp	**Pure vanilla extract**
½ Cup	**Chopped peanuts**
2 Cups	**Heavy whipping cream, whipped until stiff**

Topping:

¾ Cup	**Heavy whipping cream**
1 Cup	**Semisweet chocolate chips**
¼ Cup	**Finely chopped peanuts**

To prepare the crust: Preheat oven to 350°. Butter a 9-inch springform pan. Mix together the cookie crumbs, cinnamon, peanut butter, and melted butter. Pat over the bottom of the pan and about an inch up the sides. Bake 7 minutes. Remove from oven and cool to room temperature.

To prepare the filling: In the bowl of an electric mixer, beat the cream cheese with the powdered sugar until light and fluffy. Add the peanut butter, 2 Tbsp whipping cream, vanilla, and chopped nuts. Beat until well combined. Stir about a third of the whipped cream into the peanut butter mixture to lighten it. Gently fold in the remaining whipped cream. Pour into cooled crust and refrigerate until set, at least 2 hours.

To prepare the topping: In a small saucepan, heat the whipping cream, taking it off the heat before it boils. Pour in the chocolate chips and stir until smooth. Cool till almost room temperature, but still warm enough to pour. Remove the pie from the refrigerator. Do not remove the sides of the pan. Pour chocolate over the top of the peanut butter mixture, spreading to smooth the top. Sprinkle with finely chopped peanuts, and return pie to the refrigerator for at least another hour to let chocolate topping set. Cut with a knife warmed in hot water and wiped dry between cuts. Serve in thin slices. Store leftover pie in the refrigerator.

Make-Ahead Tip: Make dessert two days in advance; store covered in refrigerator.

1 Month Before: Plan your decorations; this is the fun part! Denim to cover the table is great and inexpensive. Bandanas from the craft stores can be used for napkins. Cowboy boots—maybe a child's size is best— from the thrift store can hold a plastic cup with water and be the vase for flowers. There are lots of great ways to decorate according to the theme; you just need to look around.

Buy and mail invitations. This is going to be a mega-event! Certainly encourage your guests to come in Western attire!!

4 Days Before: Follow up on RSVPs; verify number of guests.

3 Days Before: Gather and make ready all table linens, dishes, flatware, glasses, serving utensils, and salt and pepper grinders; plan or order centerpiece; decide on all beverages. Maybe some C & W music?

2 Days Before: Edit grocery list; shop for all items EXCEPT shrimp; purchase wines, liqueurs, and spirits.

Set the table—completely. This can be a big job if your decorations are extensive. Call a friend to help!

Prepare Creole Dipping Sauce and refrigerate in a squeeze bottle.

Make the Quick and Easy Horseradish Sauce (if serving) and refrigerate.

Make the Chocolate Peanut Butter Pie (if serving). Store tightly covered in the refrigerator.

1 Day Before: Purchase shrimp and peel them for the Coconut Shrimp; refrigerate.

Prepare the salad and refrigerate.

Prepare Spicy Peppercorn Sauce and refrigerate in a microwaveable container.

Make, and bake, the Chipotle Corn Soufflé. Refrigerate uncovered until it is completely chilled, then cover. (You don't want to hold in heat or trap condensation.)

Western Day: Grab your hat; put on your boots! (Did you know that some cornstarch sprinkled on your feet and inside your boots makes them slip on with ease?)

This timing guide will be a bit different from the others. Timing is tricky if you have only one oven (but I wrote this for single-oven kitchens). Bear with me...

This is the plan for serving:

6:00:	Guests arrive and have a cocktail
6:30:	Coconut Shrimp is served
6:45:	Cucumber, Tomato, and Onion salad is served
7:30:	Beef with Sauce and Onions, Corn Soufflé, and Green Veggie are served
8:15:	Dessert and coffee are served

4:00 or earlier: Prepare and fry the Coconut Shrimp and Frizzled Onions. For each, drain and cool on cooling racks placed over paper towel-lined sheet pans. Refrigerate uncovered on the racks (you'll use these for reheating later) until they are completely chilled, then cover.

4:45: Remove beef from refrigerator and allow it to come to room temperature.

5:15: Preheat oven to 425º. Season and sear beef.

5:30: Place green veggie in steamer basket over saucepan with water, cover, and have ready to go on the stovetop.

Place the sauce for the beef in the microwave, ready to go.

Put beef in oven to roast.

Remove cooked shrimp, corn soufflé, and onions from refrigerator.

6:30: Put shrimp in oven (with the beef) to heat for 5 minutes.

6:45: Remove beef from oven. Tent the beef with foil and let rest.

Reduce oven temperature to 350º for corn soufflé and onions.

Serve shrimp with chilled sauce.

Plate and serve salad (from the refrigerator).

Put corn soufflé in oven, covered to heat.

Turn on stovetop to steam veggie.

7:00: Put onions in the oven to heat 5-8 minutes, together with the corn soufflé.

Microwave the sauce for the beef. Remove onions and corn soufflé from the oven.

Slice thick steaks from the rib roll.

7:30: Brew coffee for dessert.

Plate the beef and top with sauce and onions. Plate the corn soufflé and the green veggie. Serve with a smile and lots of style!!

8:15: Serve dessert—either the S'mores or the Chocolate Peanut Butter Pie, and coffee.

Yippee!!! You DID it!!!
(Now about those boots and aching feet...)

Texas Cowhide Dinner

For 8 guests

Produce

☐	6 Medium	Vine-ripened tomatoes
☐	2	English cucumbers
☐		Green vegetable of your choice
☐	3 Cloves	Garlic
☐	2 Large	Onions
☐	1 Large	Red onion
☐	16 oz	Sliced button mushrooms
☐	2 Cups	Corn kernels *(fresh, or frozen and thawed)*
☐	2 Tbsp	Fresh minced Italian flat-leaf parsley
☐	2 Tbsp	Fresh minced cilantro
☐	3 Tbsp	Fresh minced chives
☐		Cilantro or parsley to garnish Corn Soufflé
☐	1 Pkg	Corn husks *(for optional containers for corn soufflé)*

Dairy & Eggs

☐	1 Cup	Unsalted butter
☐	4½ Cups	Heavy whipping cream
☐	½ Cup	Sour cream
☐	9 Large	Eggs

Cheese & Deli

☐	1½ Cups	Grated cheddar cheese
☐	4 oz	Cream cheese

Meat & Fish

☐	6 - 8 lb	Boneless beef rib roll
☐	48 Large	Raw shrimp, peeled leaving tail on, deveined

Canned Vegetables, Fruits, & Dried Fruits

☐	1¼ Cups	Beef broth
☐	1 Cup	Cream-style corn
☐	1 (4-oz) Can	Diced green chilies
☐	2	Chipotle peppers *(in adobo sauce)*

Baking, Spices, & Nuts

- ☐ ½ Cup — Sugar
- ☐ ¼ Cup — Brown sugar
- ☐ ¾ Cup — Powdered sugar
- ☐ 8 Cups — All-purpose flour
- ☐ 1 tsp — Pure vanilla extract
- ☐ 3½ Tbsp — Baking powder
- ☐ 1 Cup — Semisweet chocolate chips
- ☐ 3½ Cups — Sweetened flaked coconut
- ☐ 1 Tbsp — Cornstarch
- ☐ 5 Tbsp — Cajun seasonings
- ☐ ½ tsp — Cayenne pepper
- ☐ ½ tsp — Ground cumin
- ☐ ¾ tsp — Ground cinnamon
- ☐ ¾ Cup — Chopped peanuts

Condiments

- ☐ 6 Tbsp — Olive oil
- ☐ 96 oz — Canola oil for frying Coconut Shrimp and Frizzled Onions
- ☐ ½ Cup — Mayonnaise
- ☐ 1 Cup — Orange marmalade
- ☐ 1 Cup — Apricot preserves
- ☐ 1⅛ Cups — Smooth peanut butter
- ☐ ¼ Cup — Spicy brown mustard
- ☐ 6 Tbsp — Prepared horseradish
- ☐ ½ Cup — Apple cider vinegar
- ☐ 2 tsp — Dijon mustard
- ☐ 1 tsp — Hot sauce
- ☐ ½ Cup — Worcestershire sauce
- ☐ ½ Cup — Green peppercorns *(in a jar with brine)*
- ☐ ¼ Cup — Balsamic vinegar

Wine & Spirits

- ☐ 20 oz — Dark, full-bodied beer *(such as Shiner Bock)*
- ☐ 2 Cups — Dry red wine
- ☐ Dry Riesling for the Coconut Shrimp
- ☐ Cabernet Sauvignon for the Beef

Miscellaneous

- ☐ 1½ Cups — Crushed Oreo-type cookies *(about 24 cookies)*
- ☐ 32 — Graham cracker squares *(if making S'mores)*
- ☐ 3 (3-oz) — Gourmet chocolate bars *(if making S'mores)*
- ☐ 16 Large (or more) — Marshmallows *(if making S'mores)*

The Crowning Touch
A Dinner Fit for Royalty

Smoked Salmon and Caviar Mousse

Boston Lettuce Salad in a Parmesan Bowl

Crown Roast of Pork with Fruited Stuffing

Layered Vegetable Soufflé with
Blender Hollandaise Sauce

Orange Bowknot Rolls

Crème Brûlée with Raspberries

Meursault for the Salmon
Volnay for the Entrée

We all have very special moments in life that warrant real "ta-da" commemoration! They might be a special birthday or anniversary, a graduation or a career accomplishment, a personal triumph over adversity, or a celebration of the day and all its blessings! Occasions such as these are times to pull out all the stops—so give it all you've got and show with culinary gusto that these are truly significant events that deserve to be remembered!

Of course, we must do it all with ease and panache so that we can enjoy the revelry along with our guests. This menu comprises foods that shout, "I'm not your everyday cuisine!" At least at the Fowler house, caviar is not enjoyed on a run-of-the-mill day. This meal is all about beautiful presentation. Our salad is delicate in flavor as well as appearance and is presented to each guest in a lacy, crisp, edible bowl of golden brown Parmesan cheese. There is no need for croutons; take a bite of the bowl instead! The Crown Roast of Pork will definitely get oohs and aahs. It is majestic, especially when elegantly dressed for the occasion, with little frills perched on the tips of the rib bones. Closer inspection will reveal the aromatic stuffing, full of dried fruits glistening like the Crown Jewels. Our vegetable side dish is stunning and so easy to prepare in advance. Colorful layers of spinach, carrots, and broccoli are topped with a foolproof hollandaise sauce. The Orange Bowknot Rolls are always a part of a celebratory meal in our home. It's often a challenge to have enough left for dinner—many of these delicacies are snapped up the minute they come out of the oven. For some reason my family always feels the need for good quality control…or perhaps they are just performing their roles as Royal Tasters for the Queen. Our grand finale comes in the form of a velvety Crème Brûlée under a crunchy layer of caramelized sugar. There's more treasure to discover, though: a bottom layer of sweet, luscious raspberries. Could it get any better?

This is indeed a dinner befitting royalty or a regal occasion—and you will be amazed at how easy it is to organize and prepare in advance. This is a party you will not want to miss!

This first course is very elegant and is as tasty as it is beautiful. Let your budget determine the type of caviar you choose. Even the inexpensive grocery-store kind will impress your guests in this dish! This can be prepared a day or two in advance, making it perfect for entertaining!

Smoked Salmon and Caviar Mousse

Serves 12-15

Salmon Mixture:

8 oz	**Sliced smoked salmon** *(look for long slices)*
6 oz	**Smoked salmon** *(tidbits or slices)*
16 oz	**Cream cheese, softened**
1 Clove	**Garlic, pressed**
1 tsp	**Worcestershire sauce**
1 Tbsp	**Finely minced Italian flat-leaf parsley**

Middle Layers:

½ Cup	**Finely minced red onion**
2	**Hard-cooked eggs, peeled and finely chopped**
3 Tbsp	**Capers, drained, rinsed, and coarsely chopped**
2-4 oz	**Caviar** *(depending on your budget!)*

Lightly toasted baguette slices or buttered toast points
Parsley or dill sprigs for garnish
Lemon wedges for garnish

To prepare the salmon mixture: Spray a narrow terrine mold *(mine is 2½ x 14 inches)* or miniature loaf pans *(2 or 3, depending on size)* with vegetable oil spray. Line with plastic wrap; spray again. Line the mold with slices of smoked salmon, allowing slices to extend over the sides in order to fold over to totally encase the filling when assembly is complete. In the bowl of a food processor, combine the smoked salmon tidbits with the cream cheese, garlic, and Worcestershire sauce. Process the mixture until smooth. Quickly mix in the parsley, taking care not to overprocess.

To assemble: Spoon half of the salmon mixture into the salmon-lined mold. Sprinkle red onion evenly on top of the mixture; top with hard-cooked eggs, then capers. Place a narrow line of caviar lengthwise down the middle of the mold. Carefully spoon on the remaining half of the salmon mixture, taking care not to disturb the layers. Smooth the top. Fold in the slices of salmon extending over the sides to completely cover the filling. Give the mold a few taps on the counter to remove any air bubbles, and refrigerate the mold for several hours (or overnight) to set and firm up.

To serve: With the aid of the plastic wrap, carefully invert the terrine onto a cutting board and cut into 12 equal pieces with a very sharp knife, wiping the blade between slices. Place each slice on a chilled salad plate. Garnish with a parsley or dill sprig and a wedge of lemon. Serve chilled with toasted baguette slices or toast points.

Make-Ahead Tip: This dish can be completely assembled a day or two in advance.

Boston Lettuce

Boston lettuce is a butterhead lettuce variety, as is Bibb lettuce, and has a loosely formed head with very soft, buttery-textured leaves that are pale green to pale yellow-green. The flavor is sweet and delicate. Boston lettuce is sometimes sold with roots still attached. If this variety of lettuce is not available, substitute the tender inner leaves of leaf lettuce.

A simple salad becomes something extraordinary when served in an edible bowl. The buttery soft lettuce and the crisp Parmesan shell provide a delightful variety of textures for the palate.

Boston Lettuce Salad in a Parmesan Bowl

Serves 12

Dressing:

3 Tbsp	Honey
3 Tbsp	Lemon juice
2 Tbsp	Tarragon wine vinegar
2 Tbsp	Minced Italian flat-leaf parsley
1 Clove	Garlic, minced
1 Cup	Extra-virgin olive oil
	Salt and pepper to taste
	Shaved Parmesan cheese to garnish

Salad:

3-4 Heads	Boston lettuce, torn into bite-size pieces
1 Pint	Grape tomatoes, halved
½ Small	Red onion, very thinly sliced
⅔ Cup	Toasted pine nuts

Parmesan Bowls:

3 Cups	Shredded Parmesan cheese
4 Tbsp	All-purpose flour

To prepare the dressing: Whisk together the honey, lemon juice, vinegar, parsley, and garlic. Slowly whisk in the olive oil. Season with salt and pepper. Refrigerate until serving time.

To prepare the salad: Combine all salad ingredients and toss together with enough dressing to lightly coat the lettuce leaves. Place carefully in the cheese bowls, garnish with shaved cheese, and serve immediately.

To prepare the Parmesan bowls: Stir together the shredded cheese and the flour. Sprinkle ¼ Cup of the mixture evenly across the bottom of a small *(8- or 9-inch)* nonstick skillet. Heat over medium-high heat. Watch carefully; the cheese will first bubble up, then it will begin to brown. When it is golden brown, remove the skillet from the heat. Turn the cheese out over a 4-inch round glass bowl inverted on the counter. Carefully shape the cheese, molding it to the bowl, and allow to cool. Carefully remove. THESE ARE VERY FRAGILE! Store in an airtight container.

Make-Ahead Tip: The dressing can be prepared a day in advance and stored in the refrigerator. The Parmesan bowls can be made a day or two in advance and stored at room temperature in an airtight container. Handle carefully—they are fragile!

Expect applause when you present this regal entrée to your admiring diners. It is magnificent, but oh-so-easy to prepare. Your reign and culinary talent in the kitchen cannot be denied!

Crown Roast of Pork with Fruited Stuffing

Serves 10-12

Crown Roast :

1 (14-Rib)	Crown Roast of Pork tied by butcher, ribs frenched
8 Tbsp	Unsalted butter, melted
4 Tbsp	Herbes de Provence, or more if desired
	Salt and pepper

Fruited Stuffing:

1 Cup	Chicken broth
½ Cup	Amaretto, or other almond-flavored liqueur
½ Cup	Brandy
1 Cup	Diced dried apricots
½ Cup	Chopped dried figs
½ Cup	Chopped dried cranberries or dried cherries
1 Cup	Unsalted butter
1 Large	Onion, chopped
1 Cup	Diced celery
1 (16-oz) Pkg	Herbed seasoned stuffing (I use Pepperidge Farm)
1 Tbsp	Poultry seasoning or to taste
1 Tbsp	Minced fresh sage (optional)
2 Tbsp	Minced Italian flat-leaf parsley
2 Large	Eggs, beaten
2 Cups	Chicken broth
	Salt and pepper to taste

Pan Sauce:

1 Cup	Dry white wine
2 Tbsp	Cornstarch
1½ Cups	Chicken broth
	Salt and pepper to taste

To prepare the crown roast: Preheat oven to 425°. Remove the pork from the refrigerator about 30 minutes before placing in the oven. It will cook faster if allowed to warm up a bit. Place the crown roast in an open roasting pan. Brush with melted butter. Sprinkle generously with Herbes de Provence, salt, and pepper. Roast for 30 minutes. Lightly fill the cavity with stuffing, spooning any remaining stuffing into a greased baking dish. Reduce oven temperature to 350°, return the crown roast to the oven, and continue roasting until internal temperature reaches 155°, about 1¼-1¾ hours more. Check the temperature by inserting thermometer between rib bones, about two inches into the meat, taking care not to touch the bones. Cover stuffing with foil if it begins to get too brown. Allow roast to stand for 10-15 minutes before carving. Bake the dish of extra stuffing uncovered during the last 40 minutes the roast is in the oven.

To prepare the fruited stuffing: In a small saucepan, bring 1 Cup chicken broth, Amaretto, and brandy to a boil. Turn off heat. Add apricots, figs, and cranberries; cover, and allow fruit to plump for 30 minutes. In a large sauté pan, melt butter. Sauté the onion and celery until tender. Transfer to a large mixing bowl. Add herbed crumbs, and apricots, figs, and cranberries with their liquid. Toss lightly to combine. Add beaten eggs, 2 Cups of chicken broth, and seasonings. Combine well.

Fyi...

Herbes de Provence

This is a delicious blend of dried herbs commonly used in southern France. It usually contains basil, fennel seed, lavender flowers, marjoram, rosemary, summer savory, and thyme. It is typically used to season poultry, but can be used on other meats and vegetables. It is readily available in the spice section of most supermarkets and in gourmet stores.

Fyi...

Frenched Bones for the Crown Roast

To "french" bones, a butcher will scrape the meat and fat away from the ends of the ribs to expose the bones. These bones resemble the spires of a crown when the racks are tied in a circle.

To prepare the pan sauce: Remove the crown roast from the roasting pan and pour drippings into a fat separator. Add 4 Tbsp of fat back into the roasting pan, discarding any remaining fat but reserving the meat juices. Place the pan on top of the stove over medium-high heat and add the dry white wine, stirring the bottom of the pan to release any browned bits. Simmer until liquid is reduced by half. Dissolve the cornstarch in the chicken broth, and whisk into the pan. Continue to simmer until the mixture thickens and becomes translucent. Adjust seasonings, and serve with pork and stuffing.

Make-Ahead Tip: The stuffing can be prepared a day in advance.

I know what you're thinking…sweet rolls with a savory meal? Please don't refuse these until you've tried them. Kelly's grandmother shared this recipe with me years ago and they have become a family tradition for special occasions. They are unbelievably delicious and complement the pork roast beautifully. Trust me; I will not lead you astray!

How To …
Scald Milk

Heat milk in the microwave or on top of the stove just until you see small bubbles around the edge of the pan; this means that the milk is just under the boiling point. Be sure to cool the milk to lukewarm before combining with yeast in bread recipes.

Orange Bowknot Rolls
Makes 24

Rolls:

½ Cup	Warm water, 105°-115°
1 tsp	Sugar
1 Pkg	Active dry yeast
¾ Cup	Whole milk, scalded
½ Cup	Unsalted butter, softened
⅓ Cup	Sugar
1 tsp	Salt
2 Large	Eggs, well-beaten
¼ Cup	Orange juice
2 Tbsp	Orange zest
5-6 Cups	All-purpose flour

Orange Glaze:

3 Tbsp	Orange juice
2 Tbsp	Orange zest
1½ -2 Cups	Sifted powdered sugar

To prepare the rolls: Combine the warm water, 1 tsp sugar, and dry yeast in a medium bowl. Set aside until bubbly and foamy, up to 10 minutes. If the yeast has not bubbled, toss out and try again! In another bowl (or in the bowl of an electric mixer), combine the scalded milk, butter, ⅓ Cup sugar, and salt. Cool to lukewarm. Add yeast mixture to the milk mixture. Add eggs, orange juice, and orange zest. Beat thoroughly. Add flour in small increments and mix until it becomes a soft, but not sticky, dough. Turn dough out onto a lightly floured surface and knead until it feels smooth, elastic, and not sticky. Add more flour as needed, being sure to completely incorporate each addition before adding more. Place dough in a greased bowl and allow to rise, covered, in a warm, draft-free area until doubled in bulk (about 1-1½ hours). Punch down, removing all the air within the dough. Divide dough in half, and cut each half into 12 equal pieces. Roll each piece into an 8-inch rope. Tie each in a knot. Arrange about 2 inches apart on a greased baking sheet, or one lined with parchment paper or a Silpat. Cover with a lint-free dish towel. Allow to rise until doubled in a warm, draft-free area, about 30 minutes. Bake at 400° for about 10 minutes or until lightly browned. Drizzle with glaze while hot.

To prepare the orange glaze: Stir all glaze ingredients together until smooth. Add orange juice or more powdered sugar as needed to get a thick frosting. Spread on warm rolls.

Make-Ahead Tip: Rolls may be made and baked ahead (but not glazed!!) and frozen. Thaw and reheat in a 350° oven for 5-7 minutes. Drizzle with glaze while hot, and serve.

This is the perfect show-off side dish. It provides a bright and colorful accent on the plate and is easily prepared in advance. Who ever dreamed veggies could make such a dramatic statement?

Layered Vegetable Soufflé

Serves 12

Spinach Purée

20 oz	Frozen chopped spinach, thawed
3 Tbsp	Reserved spinach liquid
2 Large	Eggs
¼ Cup	All-purpose flour
1 Clove	Garlic, pressed
1 tsp	Lemon zest
	Salt and pepper to taste
Dash	Hot sauce

Carrot Purée

6 Medium	Carrots, peeled and sliced
1 Small	Onion, diced
1 tsp	Dried thyme leaves
	Water to cover
2 Large	Eggs
¼ Cup	All-purpose flour
	Salt and pepper to taste

Broccoli Purée

20 oz	Frozen chopped broccoli, thawed
1 Small	Onion, diced, and sautéed in a bit of oil until tender
2 Large	Eggs
¼ Cup	All-purpose flour
¼ Cup	Shredded Parmesan cheese
	Salt and pepper to taste

To prepare the spinach purée: Preheat oven to 375°. Lightly grease the bottom and sides of a 9-inch springform pan that is at least 2 inches deep. Squeeze spinach to remove excess liquid, but reserve 3 Tbsp of the liquid. In the bowl of a food processor, purée the spinach with the reserved liquid. Stir in remaining ingredients. Spread spinach purée evenly over the bottom of the pan.

To prepare the carrot purée: Place carrots, onion, and thyme in a medium saucepan with enough water to cover. Cook over medium-high heat until carrots are tender. Drain. Transfer to the bowl of a food processor, and purée. Add remaining ingredients. Carefully spread mixture over the spinach layer in the pan.

To prepare the broccoli purée: Combine all the ingredients together in the food processor, purée, and spread carefully over the carrot layer. Bake 35-40 minutes or until golden brown. Gently release sides and slice into wedges to serve.

Make-Ahead Tip: Make this a day in advance. Reheat, covered, in the oven at 350° for 15-20 minutes. Release sides, slice, and serve.

Because I once believed hollandaise sauce to be temperamental and difficult to prepare, I was reluctant to feature it in my menus. Since developing this recipe, I'm no longer hollandaise-challenged! You'll find that this foolproof method delivers creamy perfection every time.

Blender Hollandaise Sauce

Makes 1½ Cups

6	**Egg yolks, room temperature**
5 Tbsp	**Lemon juice**
	Zest of 1 large lemon
1¼ Cups	**Unsalted butter**
	Salt and white pepper
	Dash cayenne or hot sauce (optional)

Melt butter in a saucepan or in a microwave until almost boiling. In a blender or food processor, combine egg yolks, lemon juice, zest, salt, pepper, and a dash of cayenne pepper. As machine is running, very slowly add *hot* melted butter in a slow, steady stream until mixture thickens.

Make-Ahead Tip: Keep sauce warm in a preheated thermal coffee carafe for up to 1 hour before serving.

Crème Brûlée is a very popular restaurant dessert, but is easily made at home. Omit the raspberry jam and berries for a classic vanilla custard.

Crème Brûlée with Raspberries

Serves 12

1 Cup	**Raspberry jam** *(seedless is best)*
1 Pint	**Fresh raspberries**
12	**Egg yolks**
1 Cup	**Superfine sugar**
4 tsp	**Pure vanilla extract or vanilla bean paste**
4 Cups	**Heavy whipping cream**
½ Cup	**Superfine sugar or raw sugar for caramelized topping**
	Additional fresh raspberries to garnish
	Fresh mint leaves to garnish

Preheat oven to 325°. Spread about 1 Tbsp of the jam in the bottom of each (6-oz) ramekin or custard cup. I prefer the deeper ramekins to the very shallow ones. Place 5-7 raspberries in each cup on top of the jam. Whisk together the egg yolks and sugar in a large bowl. Add the vanilla extract or paste and mix well. Whisk in the whipping cream to thoroughly blend the mixture together. Gently ladle mixture over the raspberries in each cup. Bake custards in a hot water bath for about 40 minutes or until set. A knife inserted into the center will come out clean. Remove from oven. Remove ramekins from the water bath to a cooling rack and cool about 20 minutes. Refrigerate to chill completely, several hours or overnight. To prevent condensation from collecting on the tops of the custards, do not cover until they are completely chilled. A couple of hours before serving, sprinkle about ½ Tbsp superfine sugar evenly over the top of each custard. Caramelize the sugar with a kitchen torch, holding the blue part of the flame close to the sugar, and moving it back and forth in a sweeping motion. If you don't have a torch, place the ramekins in a baking pan and surround with ice to keep cold. Place about 3 inches below the broiler element and broil until sugar is melted and golden. Watch carefully; the sugar can change from a golden caramel color to burned sugar in an instant! Return ramekins to the refrigerator, uncovered, until serving time. Serve garnished with additional raspberries and a mint leaf.

Make-Ahead Tip: The Crème Brûlées can be made a day in advance; just do not top them with the sugar and caramelized until a couple of hours before serving. Store the custards tightly covered in the refrigerator.

1 Week Before: Order crown roast from butcher. Be sure to speak to a butcher, not just the person tending the meat counter.

Locate/purchase small loaf pans or terrine mold.

Purchase special decorations, unscented candles, etc.

Make and bake Orange Bowknot Rolls and freeze, unglazed, in a zip-top bag.

4 Days Before: Follow up on RSVPs; verify number of guests.

3 Days Before: Gather and make ready all table linens, dishes, a platter large enough to present the crown roast, silverware (well-polished), crystal, serving utensils (remember a carving set for the crown roast), and salt and pepper grinders; plan or order a centerpiece; decide on all beverages.

2 Days Before: Edit grocery list; shop for all items; purchase wines, liqueurs, and spirits.

Set the table—completely.

Prepare the Salmon and Caviar Mousse and refrigerate in the terrine mold, tightly covered. Prepare toasted baguette slices or toast points; store at room temperature in a zip top-bag.

Make the Parmesan cheese bowls. Store tightly covered at room temperature.

Prepare the Crème Brûlées, but do not sprinkle with sugar and caramelize. Refrigerate tightly covered.

1 Day Before: Prepare Fruited Stuffing and refrigerate.

Make the salad dressing; refrigerate. Toast the pine nuts; store at room temperature. Wash Boston lettuce, spin dry and store in a zip-top bag in the refrigerator. Prepare vegetables for the salad and store separately in the refrigerator. Shave Parmesan cheese and store in a tightly covered container.

Prepare and bake the Layered Vegetable Soufflé. After it cools, refrigerate uncovered until completely chilled. Cover tightly.

Place frozen rolls in the refrigerator to thaw. Do not unzip the bag!

Coronation Day: Sound the Trumpets!

Mid-morning: Stir together the glaze for the rolls. Cover and refrigerate.
Slice and plate Smoked Salmon and Caviar Mousse, garnish with dill and

lemon wedge. Cover and refrigerate. Add baguette slices immediately before serving.

4 Hours Before: Remove crown roast from refrigerator and place in a roasting pan. Brush with butter and season. Remove Fruited Stuffing from refrigerator.

3½ Hours Before: Preheat oven to 425° for the crown roast.

3 Hours Before: Place crown roast in the oven; set timer for 30 minutes.

2½ Hours Before: Reduce oven temperature to 350°; fill cavity of roast with stuffing; return to oven.

Place Parmesan cheese bowls on salad plates.

1 Hour Before: Remove Layered Vegetable Soufflé from the refrigerator.

Prepare Hollandaise Sauce and keep warm in a heated thermal carafe.

Remove thawed rolls from the refrigerator and place on a baking sheet. Put orange glaze to sit at room temperature.

Sprinkle Crème Brûlées with sugar and caramelize. Return uncovered to the refrigerator.

45 Minutes Before: Check roast temperature. When done, remove to serving platter, tent with foil to keep warm. Pour off drippings and proceed with pan sauce, keep warm. Place baking dish with extra stuffing in the oven.

Remove Salmon and Caviar Mousse plates from the refrigerator and add baguette slices.

30 Minutes Before: Preheat oven to 350° (or place in the same oven used for the pork) to reheat the Layered Vegetable Soufflé and Orange Bowknot Rolls. Allow about 20 minutes for the Vegetable Soufflé to heat, and 5-7 minutes for the rolls; glaze while hot out of the oven.

Brew coffee.

Show time! Serve the Salmon and Caviar Mousse.

Toss lettuce and vegetables with dressing and carefully mound in the bowls. Garnish with shaved Parmesan. Serve.

Slice and plate Vegetable Soufflé, drizzle with Hollandaise. Serve additional stuffing on plates.

Present Crown Roast, and carve at the table. Eat and enjoy with Pan Sauce.

Serve dessert and coffee.

Decree this celebration a delicious success!

Enjoy your days...Love your life!

The Crowning Touch
A Dinner Fit for Royalty

For 10-12 People

Produce

☐	7	Lemons *(including 2 to garnish Salmon and Caviar Mousse)*
☐	3	Oranges
☐	2 Pints	Fresh raspberries
☐	3 Large	Onions
☐	2 Small	Red onions
☐	3 Cloves	Garlic
☐	1 Pint	Grape tomatoes
☐	3-4 Heads	Boston lettuce
☐	3-4 Stalks	Celery
☐	6 Medium	Carrots
☐	5 Tbsp	Finely minced Italian flat-leaf parsley
☐	1 Tbsp	Minced fresh sage
☐		Fresh dill to garnish Salmon and Caviar Mousse
☐		Fresh mint to garnish Crème Brûlée

Dairy & Eggs

☐	3¼ Cups	Unsalted butter
☐	¾ Cup	Whole milk
☐	4 Cups	Heavy whipping cream
☐	30 Large	Eggs

Cheese & Deli

☐	16 oz	Cream cheese
☐	4 oz	Parmesan cheese, block type
☐	3¼ Cups	Shredded Parmesan cheese

Meat & Fish

☐	1 (14-rib)	Crown Roast of Pork tied by the butcher, ribs frenched
☐	8 oz	Sliced smoked salmon
☐	6 oz	Smoked salmon (tidbits or slices)

Canned Vegetables, Fruits, & Dried Fruits

☐	4½ Cups	Chicken broth

☐ 1 Cup   Diced dried apricots
☐ ½ Cup   Chopped dried figs
☐ ½ Cup   Chopped dried cranberries or dried cherries

Pasta, Grains, Cereal
☐ 1 (16-oz) Pkg   Herbed seasoned stuffing *(I use Pepperidge Farm)*

Baking, Spices, & Nuts
☐ 7 Cups   All-purpose flour
☐ ½ Cup   Sugar
☐ 1½ -2 Cups   Sifted powdered sugar
☐ 1½ Cups   Superfine sugar
☐ 3 Tbsp   Honey
☐ 4 tsp   Pure vanilla extract or vanilla bean paste
☐ 2 Tbsp   Cornstarch
☐ 1 Pkg   Active dry yeast
☐ 4 Tbsp   Herbes de Provence
☐ 1 Tbsp   Poultry seasoning
☐ 1 tsp   Dried thyme leaves
☐ ⅔ Cup   Pine nuts

Condiments
☐ 1 Cup   Extra-virgin olive oil
☐ 2 Tbsp   Tarragon wine vinegar
☐ 1 tsp   Worcestershire sauce
☐ 3 Tbsp   Capers
☐ 2-4 oz   Caviar
☐ Dash   Hot sauce
☐ 1 Cup   Raspberry jam *(seedless is best)*

Breads
☐ 2   Baguettes *(to accompany Salmon and Caviar Mousse)*

Freezer
☐ 20 oz   Frozen chopped spinach
☐ 20 oz   Frozen chopped broccoli

Wine & Spirits
☐ ½ Cup   Amaretto *(or other almond-flavored liqueur)*
☐ ½ Cup   Brandy
☐ 1 Cup   Dry white wine
☐   Meursault or a Full-Bodied Chardonnay and Volnay or a Full-Bodied Pinot Noir

Index

A

Accompaniments
Apricot Sauce, 82
Dijon Sauce, 22
Dill Dip, Easy, 12
Gravy, 67
Herbed Cheese Topping, 16
Herbed Crumb Topping, 26
Hollandaise Sauce, Blender, 166
Horseradish Sauce, 146
Kahlúa Sauce, 29
Lime Cream, 96
Marinade, 82, 142
Peppercorn Sauce, 144
Raspberry Coulis, 132
Salsa, Kevin's Roasted, 94
Spicy Creole Dipping Sauce, 141
Tapenade, 16
Wine Shallot Sauce, 38

Appetizers
Blue Cheese Mousse, 11
Brie and Pear Quesadillas, 10
Bruschetta with Herbed Cheese and
    Tapenade 16
Coconut Shrimp with Spicy Creole Dipping
    Sauce, 141
Easy Dill Dip for Vegetable Crudites, 12
Kevin's Roasted Salsa, 94
Killer Chile con Queso, 13
Shrimp Dijon, 14
Spicy Party Nuts, 15
Smoked Salmon and Caviar Mousse, 157
Proscuitto Palmiers, 9
Apple and Romaine Salad, 80
Apple Pie in a Sack, 70
Artichoke Salad, Curried Chicken and, 126
Asparagus, Oven-Roasted, 41
Asparagus, Shrimp Louis on, 125

B

Banana Bread Pudding with Kahlúa Sauce,
    28-29
Beets, Salad of, and Panko-Crusted Goat
Cheese with Lemon Vinaigrette, 128
Beverages-
Kevin's Margaritas, 93
Mike's Drink, 21
Boston Lettuce Salad in a Parmesan Bowl, 158
Breads-
Bruschetta with Herbed Cheese and
    Tapenade, 16
Orange Bowknot Rolls, 162
Quick-Rise Dinner Rolls with Herbed Butter,
    130
Tony's Toast, 55
Brie and Pear Quesadillas, 10

Brisket, Molly's, 112
Broccoli Salad, 111
Mexican Brownies, 102
Butternut Bisque, 79

C

Caesar Salad, Molly's Sensational, 51
Carrots, Oven-Glazed, 67
Carrot Cake, Our Favorite, 85
Caviar Mousse, Smoked Salmon and, 157
Cheese Herbed, Bruschetta with, and Tapenade,
    16
Cheese, Panko-Crusted Goat, in Salad of Beets
    with Lemon Vinaigrette, 128
Chicken, Curried, and Artichoke Salad, 126
Chicken Enchiladas, Green Chile, 101
Chicken, Perfect Roast with Gravy, 67
Chile con Queso, Killer, 13
Chipotle Corn Soufflé, 147
Chocolate Mousse, Elegant, with Raspberry
    Coulis, 132
Chocolate Peanut Butter Pie, 149
Chocolate Sheath Cake, Monte's, 117
Coconut Shrimp with Spicy Creole Dipping
    Sauce, 141
Corn Soup, Roasted, with Lime Cream, 96
Coulis, Raspberry, 132
Crème Brûlée with Raspberries, 167
Crown Roast of Pork with Fruited Stuffing, 160

D

Desserts-
Apple Pie in a Sack, 70
Banana Bread Pudding with Kahlúa Sauce,
    28-29
Brownies, Mexican, 102
Carrot Cake, Our Favorite, 85
Chocolate Peanut Butter Pie, 149
Chocolate Mousse, Elegant, with Raspberry
    Coulis, 132
Chocolate Sheath Cake, Monte's, 117
Crème Brûlée with Raspberries, 167
Tiramisu, 56
Tropical Tart, 42
Dijon Sauce, Scotch Eggs with, on Mixed
    Greens, 22
Dressing-
Celery Vinaigrette, 37
Cumin Vinaigrette, 126
Greek Goddess Dressing, 65
Lemon Vinaigrette, 128
Vinaigrette, 80

E

Easy Dill Dip for Vegetable Crudites – p. 12

Enchiladas, Green Chile Chicken, 101

F

FYI's –
Al dente, 52
Boston lettuce, 158
Buy the best, 21
Chipotle peppers, 147
Créme Frîche, 79
English cucumbers, 142
French bones for the Crown Roast, 161
Fresh Serano chilies, 10
Fresh Spinach, 54
Herbes de Provence, 161
How much flour for bread making, 131
Jicama, 98
Juice and zest yields from lemons and limes,
    65
Meat and Marinade, 82
Panko crumbs, 129
Peel and dice butternut squash, 79
Puff pastry vs Phyllo Dough, 9
Removable-bottom tart pans, 42
Rising Bread, 130
Shallots, 38
Tomatillos, 94
Use of raw egg yokes, 65

G

Gravy, 67
Green Beans with Herbed Crumb Topping, 26
Green Chile Chicken Enchiladas, 101

H

Herbed Crumb Topping, Green Beans with, 26
Herb-Sautéed Vegetables, 84
Hollandaise Sauce, Blender, Layered Vegetable
    Soufflé with, 166
Horseradish Sauce, Quick and Easy, 146
How to's-
Buy and prepare leeks, 25
Buy, use, and store fresh gingerroot, 82
Cook asparagus tender-crisp, 125
Cook boneless, skinless chicken breast halves,
    126
Cook shrimp, 14
Create corn husk containers for Chipotle Corn
    Soufflé, 147
Hard-cook an egg, 22
Hints and tips for working with chicken, 66
Make homemade croutons, 51
Make Make nuts pretty for topping, 148
Make soft, fresh bread crumbs, 26
Make chocolate cup for mousse, 132
Scald milk, 162

Store oils, 80
Toast nuts, 28

I, J
Jicama, 98

K
Kahlúa Sauce, Banana Bread Pudding with, 29

L
Lettuce, Boston, Salad in a Parmesan Bowl, 158
Leeks and Tomatoes, Ricotta Tart with, 25

M
Margaritas, Kevin's, 93
Manicotti, 52
Meats-
   Crown Roast of Pork with Fruited Stuffing, 160
   Curried Chicken and Artichoke Salad, 126
   Green Chile Chicken Enchiladas, 101
   Grilled Rib Roll with Spicy Peppercorn Sauce, 144
   Marinated Pork Tenderloin with Herb-Sautéed Vegetables, 82
   Molly's Brisket, 112
   Perfect Roast Chicken with Gravy, 67
Mexican Brownies, 102
Molly's Mashed Potatoes or Rosemary-Roasted New Potatoes, 68
Mousse, Blue Cheese, 11
Mousse, Elegant Chocolate with Raspberry Coulis, 132
Mousse, Smoked Salmon and Caviar, 157

N
Nuts, Spicy Party, 15
Pecans on Mixed Greens, Salad of Pear, Roquefort, and, 37

O
Onions, Frizzled, 143
Onion Salad, Marinated Cucumber, Tomato, and, 142
Orange Bowknot Rolls, 162

P
Parmesan Bowl, Boston Lettuce Salad in a, 158
Pasta-
   Manicotti, 52
Peanut Butter Pie, Chocolate, 149
Pecans on Mixed Greens, Salad of Pear, Roquefort, and, 37
Peppercorn Sauce, Spicy on Grilled Rib Roll, 144

Pie, Apple, in a Sack, 70
Pork Tenderloin, Marinated, with Herb-Sautéed Vegetables, 82
Pork, Crown Roast of, with Fruited Stuffing, 160
Potatoes, Molly's Mashed or Rosemary-Roasted New Potatoes, 68
Proscuitto Palmiers, 9

Q
Quesadillas, Brie and Pear, 10
Quick-Rise Dinner Rolls with Herbed Butter, 130

R
Raspberries-
   Raspberries, Crème Brûlée with, 167
   Raspberry Coulis, Elegant Chocolate Mousse with, 132
Rice, Creamy Lemon, 40
Rice, Green Chile, 114
Rib Roll, Grilled, with Spicy Peppercorn Sauce, 144
Rosemary-Roasted New Potatoes, 68
Rolls, Orange Bowknot, 162
Rolls, Quick-Rise Dinner, with Herbed Butter, 130
Ricotta Tart with Leeks and Tomatoes, 25
Roquefort, and Pecans on Mixed Greens, Salad of Pear, 37

S
Salads-
   Apple and Romaine Salad, 80
   Boston Lettuce Salad in a Parmesan Bowl, 158
   Broccoli Salad, 111
   Curried Chicken and Artichoke Salad, 126
   Marinated Cucumber, Tomato, and Onion Salad, 142
   Molly's Sensational Caesar Salad, 51
   Salad of Beets and Panko-Crusted Goat Cheese with Lemon Vinaigrette, 128
   Salad of Pear, Roquefort, and Pecans on Mixed Greens, 37
   Salad with Greek Goddess Dressing, 65
   Salsa, Kevin's Roasted, 94
   South of the Border Salad with Cumin Vinaigrette, 98
Salmon Smoked, and Caviar Mousse, 157
Sauces-
   Apricot Sauce, 82
   Blender Hollandaise Sauce, Layered Vegetable Soufflé with, 164
   Dijon Sauce on Scotch Eggs, with Mixed Greens, 22
   Kahlúa Sauce, Banana Bread Pudding with, 29
   Quick and Easy Horseradish Sauce, 146

   Spicy Peppercorn Sauce, Grilled Rib Roll with, 144
   Wine-shallot Sauce, Pan-Seared Salmon on Spinach with, 38
Shrimp-
   Coconut Shrimp with Spicy Creole Dipping Sauce, 141
   Shrimp Dijon, 14
   Shrimp Louis on Asparagus, 125
S'mores, Over-the-Top Tableside, 148
Soufflés-
   Soufflé, Chipotle Corn, 147
   Soufflé, Layered Vegetable with Blender Hollandaise Sauce, 164, 166
Soup-
   Butternut Bisque, 79
   Corn Soup, Roasted with Lime Cream, 96
Spicy Party Nuts, 15
Spinach. Garlic-Sautéed, 54
Stuffing, Fruited, Crown Roast of Pork with, 160

T
Tarts-
   Ricotta Tart with Leeks and Tomatoes, 25
   Tropical Tart, 42
Tiramisu, 56
Tony's Toast, 55
Topping Herbed Crumb, Green Beans with, 26

U, V
Vegetables-
   Artichoke Salad, Curried Chicken and, 126
   Broccoli Salad, 111
   Creamy Lemon Rice – p. 40
   Frizzled Onions – p. 143
   Green Beans with Herbed Crumb Topping, 26
   Herb-Sautéed Vegetables, 84
   Layered Vegetable Soufflé with Blender Hollandaise Sauce, 164, 166
   Molly's Mashed Potatoes or Rosemary Roasted New Potatoes, 68
   Oven-Glazed Carrots, 67
   Oven-Roasted Asparagus, 41
   Salad of Beets and Panko-Crusted Goat Cheese with Lemon Vinaigrette, 128
   Spinach, Garlic-Sautéed, 54
Vinaigrette, Cumin, South of the Border Salad with, 98

W, X, Y, Z
Pan-Seared Salmon on Spinach with Wine shallot Sauce, 38
Zest, 65, 26

Recipe Testers

Rhonda Barhorst
Peggy Bush-Everding
Ann Carter Curran
Chris Cobb
Barbara Coffey
Jill Crain
Mary Jane Doster
Shirley Fisher
Ingrid Forrieter
Karen Handschy
Angela Hobby
Iris Horton
Ellie Johnston
Leslie Hobbs King
Liz Lusk
Trish Matthews
Barbara Meriam
Terri Mertz
Diane Moore
Terri Parris
Jenny Proznik
Lory Quist
Pat Sheets
Jill Spears
Judy Swerer